My Teacher Life

Why Make Your Own Mistakes When You Can Learn from Mine?

By

Ingrid U. Hearn

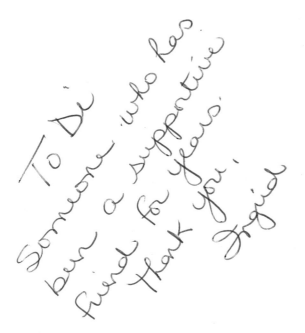

To Di
Someone who has
been a supportive
friend for years.
Thank you.
Ingrid

ISBN: 1-4033-8784-2 (e-book)
ISBN: 1-4033-8785-0 (Paperback)

Library of Congress Control Number: 2002095302

This book is printed on acid free paper.

Printed in the United States of America
Bloomington, IN

1stBooks - rev. 12/23/02

FOREWORD

If you are a new teacher entering the profession or if you are one who just needs some motivation and encouragement, then this could be the book for you! After researching countless books written for teachers, I have found that there are some amazing resource books filled to the brim with useable charts and lists, sporting colorful cartoons and photographs, and providing countless theme units and lesson plans. I could not provide you with a more beneficial or accurate resource book than what I have seen on the shelves already. This book is not about that!

There are "helpful hints" books, providing "step by step" instructions on "how to teach" reading, mathematics, science, geography etc. This book is not about that, either. There are scientifically researched books dedicated to the various techniques used to teach to the different learning styles of boys and girls. Nope, not this one. Finally, there are books of all shapes and great thicknesses, coordinated in vivid color and bound with beautiful coils. Again, nothing fancy here. My book is meant to be quite different!

For lack of a better description, this book is written as a non-fiction, educational self help book that gets "up close and personal". It should cause you to pause and reflect and take a good look at yourself and the career that you have chosen. It is meant to provide you with some enlightening, yet light-hearted reading. My hope is that it will inspire you with the desire to become the best you can be and then to pass that on to children, more explicitly, those whom you teach. It does not provide a lot of well-laid out charts or samples of lesson plans, but it does present useful teaching strategies and the reasons for their success. It expresses a candid view of life's experiences, both good and bad, allowing you to feel "normal" and "okay" when things go wrong. Please accept my sincerest desires for you to be GREAT and allow me into your life for but a brief time in order that I may convince you of how truly great you are and to point out some of the life-changing experiences you can provide for those children who are anxiously waiting for you.

Had anyone ever decided to plan an Oscar night for teachers, it would have eventually proven an effort in futility. The "categories" rubric would have been pages long requiring a team of experts to document sufficient criteria and headings. The list of categories would have been endless because it is common knowledge among educators and children that those who teach are generally super heroes who can perform almost any task effortlessly and endlessly. The list of candidates would have become astronomical because...how many good teachers are there? Had winners actually been chosen, their acceptance speeches would have been so eloquent and informative that it would be difficult to curb their "time" and begin the music.

The solution, of course, is to let you in on a well-kept secret. "Teachers; you are all worthy of an Oscar." Even though there is no special night and no fancy statue, there is the knowledge that you, the teacher, are doing something wonderful and miraculous in the lives of children by guiding them through a year or two of their journey.

With this in mind, I would like you to sit back and relax as you catch a glimpse into the life of a "born" teacher, one who has always loved children and who has always had a true desire to make a positive difference in their lives.

Let it be understood that I am certainly not the "world expert" on the subject of teaching. In trying to provide positive direction for approximately three thousand students, I have learned a great deal about myself and the art of teaching over the past 30 years.

I continue to love it and would like to share some of my more important learning experiences with you who have also chosen this profession.

I would very much have appreciated the candid written voice of a more experienced teacher when I began my journey into the field of education. I believe that the pupils of my early years would have been spared some of the negative learning experiences that I imposed upon them by virtue of my ignorance.

"Regrets? I've had a few - but then again, too few to mention."

This line from Dean Martin's song has always been one of my favorites. We can't progress if we dwell upon regrets; we must move forward. By sharing my insights, I hope to help you move forward with perhaps less regrets than I have had.

Have I made mistakes? Too many to remember - but certainly enough of them to know that I have gained a great deal of knowledge and experience from them. That, I have learned, is one of the keys to achieving success.

The secret here is to always realize and accept your mistakes. Be willing to learn from them. Always be humble enough to realize that you are capable of making mistakes just as every human who is in the learning flux does. If you can grasp this, you are in the company of many great philosophers, inventors, world leaders, and the like.

It is a well known fact that we, as humans, learn from mistakes, whether they be our own or those made by others. (Obviously, the latter is a much better way to go.) I will therefore willingly share some of my mistakes in order for you to learn from them and perhaps avoid having to experience them firsthand.

Not only should you understand the "learning from mistakes" fact, but children need to learn and know this! It should be one of the main topics at the beginning of each school year.

This book was written for YOU. It is a compilation of valuable insights derived from many people over the course of my lifetime. It will give you direction, allow you freedom from much of your self-inflicted guilt and shed some insights with true life examples. I share Napoleon Hill's Plan for Success and how easily it relates to the teaching profession.

I have made every effort to create a multi-faceted book; a reference book at times, a comfort when things are not going as well as planned and a bit of light-hearted entertainment along that wonderful path to becoming the best teacher you can be.

Dedication

This book is dedicated to the most important people in my life: my husband Dan, who has been my greatest advocate and supporter and who has been influential in providing me with much of the material in this book, my children Ashlie, Jeremy and Rebecca who have taught me about true love, patience and understanding and who have lived through many of my challenges (even creating a few of their own "to help me stretch and grow"), to my good friends and family members who have significantly promoted and supported my profession and encouraged me to compile my experiences in a book, and to my mom who has been my most faithful lifetime friend and often believes in me even more than I do.

Together, they have been the reliable force in supporting my fulfilling, precious career - that of being a teacher.

TABLE OF CONTENTS

INTRODUCTION
"There are many reasons for writing a book. Mine is simple. I wish to give something back. So many people have influenced me. So many children have shared their love of learning with me and have taught me about the different worlds that we live in. They have provided me with a wonderful education and now I wish to share it with you.

CHAPTER ONE
Do you wish to be Successful?
Napoleon Hill's Plan for Success - Steps to follow
There is a definite pattern and it works!

CHAPTER TWO
Why are you Here?
Taking a serious look at your motives and goals

CHAPTER THREE
Can you Handle Criticism?
Preparing yourself for the world of scrutiny and advice

CHAPTER FOUR
What is Your Job?
Definition and outline of what the expectations are
A No-fail Recipe for Teaching Children
The Learning Game - Two approaches to learning - a factual list
Imagination is Vital

CHAPTER FIVE
You Can Make it if you Try
Strategies to make the workload easier to handle
Blending subjects and materials

CHAPTER SIX
Developing Good Habits for Yourself
Teaching good habits in the classroom and reasons why they should be instilled at an early age
"Consciousness" and its importance
Formula for successful studying

CHAPTER SEVEN
Building Confidence in the Classroom
The difference between self-esteem and confidence
A list of strategies to build confidence
Reasonable risks and why we should take them (Do you own a chenille bathrobe?)

CHAPTER EIGHT
Don't Re-Invent the Wheel
Learn to find and utilize available resources
Tapping into a wealth of knowledge
Share! Share! Share!

CHAPTER NINE
Planning
Plan for yourself
Long Range plans
The Daybook and its function
How to plan effectively

CHAPTER TEN
Mistakes - I'll Make a Few
Understanding that mistakes are a natural part of the learning process - a few examples
Instilling this belief in your students is vital
Mother Ease and its effectiveness in the classroom

CHAPTER ELEVEN
Classroom Management
Strategies that have worked in creating a manageable group
Crowd control
School trips and tips

CHAPTER EIGHTEEN
Celebrate! Celebrate!
Any excuse will do
Ideas on how to celebrate

CHAPTER NINETEEN
Accentuate the Positive!
Who makes the impressions
A personal example
How have you been affected?

CHAPTER TWENTY
Tragedy in the Classroom
Ways in which to deal with difficult situations in the classroom
How students deal with death
Strategies to help you cope

CHAPTER TWENTY-ONE
Go the Extra Mile
Why should we?
A Personal Insight and testimony

CHAPTER TWENTY-TWO
Building Self Esteem
From the Experts
Children have to follow the rules
Winner and Loser thoughts
An inspiring example of a winner
Are we our Labels?
Actual Lessons and Games to Use in the Classroom

CONCLUSION
Let's Wrap it up!
That's all there is for now - but...
List of Research Books you may wish to read

INTRODUCTION

Congratulations!!!!! You have chosen one of the most difficult, challenging and rewarding careers on the planet. I would suppose that you fall into the category of the kid who has always loved school and wish to be a student for the rest of your professional life.

Yes- I did say student! An important expression that I learned from the famous psychologist Don Wolfe is that "the more you know, the more you will realize how little you know."

You will continue to have many teachers in your life, including each and every one of your students, their parents, your peers, school boards, federation, and, of course, your own children. (should you still choose to have them after your first few years of teaching)

It is important to note that you will have to take great care when naming your offspring because the name you choose could conjure up a vision of that horrific behavior problem that you had to live with each day of school in 1995 (these children are NEVER absent) or the unforgettable parent who berated you in the staffroom in front of your peers on Monday, June 3, 1996 at 12:22 p.m.

Yes, you are entering the "Education Zone"- a place for the courageous who, with limitless effort, fight the evils of apathy, negativity and poor self-esteem on a daily; no hourly basis. Get out the tights and cape and hang on. This is the stuff that futures are made of.

If you are ready, you will enjoy the roller coaster ride of a lifetime because it can be a thrilling and exhilarating experience; or not. "May the force be with you."

In the chapters following this introduction, I will outline, explain, clarify and share some of the hurtles, questions, examples and learning experiences that have crossed the minds and lives of myself and others in this profession.

The most important thing to stress is that you must always be receptive to learning. Take courses, read self-improvement books and be willing to listen to the valuable experiences of other teachers in order to constantly learn and grow. This journey will never end. It may take other paths but, once you are a teacher, you will always be a teacher.

Let the journey begin.

CHAPTER ONE

Do You Wish to be Successful?

Contrary to popular belief, there are certain steps you must take in order to become successful.

Many people believe that you are "lucky" or "you were in the right place at the right time". These thoughts are very common but the truth of the matter is that **you** are responsible for making those "lucky" things happen and **you** are at the "right place at the right time" by virtue of your thoughts and goals.

The following chapter is derived from the teachings of Napoleon Hill, a very profound, very wealthy man who studied with Andrew Carnegie and interviewed many famous people including Thomas Jefferson, Thomas Edison and the like. I believe that he truly exemplified what he taught and I have used much of his philosophy in my life. It works! He is no longer with us but he has left a huge legacy in his books and in the millionaires he has helped to create. His philosophies can be translated for every career and I have blended much of his teachings to suit the education field.

There are definite steps that you must take to be successful. You must begin with **the DREAM**. The dream is what you envision for yourself right now. It can't be vague and must include exactly those things that you wish to see for yourself.

Do you see yourself as a successful coach? A music director? A French teacher? A principal? Focus on that dream, see it in your mind, talk it out to yourself, and you will become it. Your dream can change or take another form sometime in the future, but **find your dream for now**!

I would like to begin this chapter with a poem that Napoleon Hill wrote in his book, "Think and Grow Rich". My husband has read it to me many times over the past few years and I have come to realize its truth. It is thought provoking and lends itself well to the next few pages.

"I bargained with Life for a penny,
And life would pay no more,
However I begged at evening
When I counted my scanty store.

For life is just an employer,
He gives you what you ask,
But once you set the wages,
Why you must bear the task.

I worked for a menial's hire,
Only to learn, dismayed
That any wage I asked of Life,
Life would have willingly paid."

Are we asking for what we are worth? Are we willing to accept the mediocre? Read on and accept nothing less than the true desires of your heart and **SUCCESS.**

PLAN FOR SUCCESS

Napoleon Hill's plan for success can be considered generic. It was not created for the teaching profession, but, because it is such a vital part of any goal setting process, I have included it in this book. No matter which profession you choose, if followed properly, this plan of success will help you to accomplish it.

(1) The first thing that you must have is a **definiteness of purpose**. You must turn your will power on to high and not accept defeat. Create in writing your own aims and purpose and then go on to create your own circumstances.

Purpose -find your definiteness of purpose

Plan -create a definite plan for its achievement. What are the steps necessary to achieve your purpose? Write them down. Short-term goals come first, followed by long-term goals and how they can be achieved.

Action-It follows the old adage that we already know "Faith without works is dead."

"There will be no success if there is no definiteness of purpose."
Napoleon Hill

Wishing for something is not enough. You must back your purpose with everything you have because your purpose must become a part of your subconscious. If it does not, it cannot be a part of you. If your purpose is to become the best Kindergarten teacher or Vice-Principal the Board has ever seen, then eat, sleep and believe it.

In other words, you must think about your purpose regularly, repeat it to yourself out loud and discuss it with your friends. (Not at nauseam but in true belief)

It is important to make this goal a part of who you are and what you do because quite frankly, once the decision is made, there is no turning back. The life of an educator becomes **your** lifestyle.

An Example

While going about your business during your usual shopping trip to the mall, you will begin to automatically zone in on useful classroom items with your "teacher-sonar". You'll become aware of inexpensive, colorful stickers and positive reinforcements that have never been there before. An amazing array of books will jump out at you as they become contenders for the resource unit that you are putting together.

Your friends may leave you in the "resource section" of the department store and continue on with their own search of fishing gear or the perfect outfit that you both need for that big party on the weekend. If they are your true friends, they will be unusually understanding and even take on the role of "accomplice" in acquiring exotic resources for those "different" lessons. The weekly visit to the Dollar Store will undoubtedly become a ritual and minor changes in your life will occur gradually as you incorporate this profession into every facet of your being.

Stay calm! This is a natural occurrence and can only lead you to certain success as a teacher.

(2)**All individual achievements** are the results of a motive or a combination of motives. There are 9 altogether. The first three motives in the list are the greatest motives for persons to strive for success. Unfortunately, the teaching profession does not lend itself well to the third motive but there are more in the list that can drive you to teach.

a) **emotion of love**

I sincerely hope that the love "of and for" children is one of the main factors that has brought you here. It is a great motive for becoming an amazing teacher. If you have this "love", you will be successful in the eyes of children and their parents because this emotion will be evident in all of your decision making.

b) emotion of sex

Although not directly related to teaching, it is a major component of the drive for success and, as I would like to present this material in its entirety, I have included it as part of the list. It could...nah.

c) desire for material wealth

Again, not a particularly serious motive for teaching because, contrary to popular public belief, teachers do not rank among the "rich and famous".

I do believe however, that stability, a steady paycheck and good benefits do amount to material wealth in the eyes of many. You will have these things as a result of signing a permanent contract with a Board of Education.

d) the desire for self-preservation

This is a driving force **during** your career

e) the desire for freedom of body and mind

This is an excellent desire for the yoga practicing, Phys. Ed. Teacher. In all seriousness, be sure to find a stress- reliever in some type of exercise or physical fitness routine. It is a necessary component of staying healthy in any career.

f) the desire for personal recognition and expression

Hopefully this is one of the more important motives that has brought you here. It fulfills your own goals as well as creating an enriched environment for your students. They will automatically begin to share your love of learning.

g) perpetuation of life after death

A cool thing to realize here is that upon your death, your ideas and teachings will live on in the students you touch. I don't think that Mr. Hill meant this, but it fits. My high school principal, Mr. Ernie Grove, was one of the greatest positive influences in my teenage life. The wonderful memory of his love and dedication to his career has most definitely lived on in his students. I will remember him always. Thank you, Mr. Grove!

Again, I realize that some of these motives may seem to have very little to do with your decision to become a teacher but I feel compelled to share Napoleon Hill's philosophy in its entirety. As he explains, the last two motives to complete the list are very negative ones whereas the first seven were of a more positive nature and, of course, more beneficial.

h) desire for revenge

I could become very catty here and bring politicians into the picture but, of course, I won't because this book is not about that. You may be able to decide for yourself the damage that can be done when negative forces are used as motives. Revenge more often hurts the perpetrator than the victim.

i) emotion of fear   I would like to address this emotion in the following paragraphs

Fear is one of the strongest emotions that we feel. We often face the fear of failure or the fear of rejection. You will encounter this "fear" in the teaching profession and, as I have felt it at times, I would like to teach you how to deal with it. Burke Hedges, author of "You Inc.", writes that "the key to managing fear is to face it head on, not to put on a brave face and pretend it doesn't exist."

We're all afraid sometimes; fear is a natural human component. Too many people try to avoid fear by hiding from it.

"A ship in harbor is safe. But that's not what ships are built for."

By refusing to take risks, you are not managing fear. Fear then manages you and controls your life. Many athletes and entertainers have often expressed their feelings of nervousness and fear prior to a performance. Their success is achieved by managing their emotions and using them to enhance their performance.

Helen Hayes, a very famous actor whose career spanned over 60 years, was quoted as saying "Of course, I get scared up there. But I don't think of fear as a deterrent. I think of it as a kick in the rear to prepare."

Fears play an incredible role in the decisions that we make and they often motivate people for right or wrong. The self-talk that goes on inside your head controls the course that your life will take. When you fill your brain with negative thoughts, your path will become less successful than when you fill your head with positive, self-building conversation. The more we learn about the power of the brain, the more we must realize that it requires positive direction. It will follow our instructions, no matter what they may be.

Example: "I would never be able to become a principal." You have now instructed your brain to disallow you from becoming a principal and it will follow the instructions you have given it. That is it's job.

THERE ARE ALL TYPES OF FEAR

There are various types of fears, each playing a significant role in the success or failure of the lives they impact.

1) **fear of poverty**   You must become **success conscious** and not allow yourself to have limitations put upon you, either by your own self or by another person.

2) **fear of criticism**   We have often heard it said that we cannot do that because "they" will disapprove or "they" won't accept it?

Does anyone know who "they" are? I have not yet figured out who "they" are.

There are certain people that we must be accountable to. These are distinct people with names and positions but the "they" that is commonly referred to is an imaginary group which sets limitations upon us.

"They" destroy imagination, stupefy enthusiasm, cut down personal initiative, and create mediocrity which cannot be overcome. In this life, in order to be successful, you must not be ordinary. Allow yourself the luxury of ignoring the "theys" of the world and "fly".

If I had allowed myself to worry about the "theys" of the world, I would not have had the courage to write this book. If you fear criticism, you have lost the battle before it has begun. This is where you rely upon your friends, allowing them to be the voice of encouragement. My friend Richelle has taught me many things in life, one of them is to "be yourself" and to attempt new things. She has always been a solid and true friend who has given her honest opinion when it's needed. I have tapped into that "real resource" many times and ignored the fear of "the unknown theys."

Thanks, Richelle, for always being there to encourage me!

8

3) **fear of ill-health**   Many people create this fear in themselves and can reach the point of "hypochondriac," a label given to those who envision themselves suffering constantly from ill-health. This becomes a very debilitating fear as it can create the illnesses that one believes he/she is suffering from. The mind is a powerful thing. With repeated discussion , it can and will create them. This is a very serious truth.

"Talk Health. The dreary never-ending tale
Of mortal maladies is worn and stale;
You cannot charm or interest or please
By harping on that minor chord, disease.
Say you are well, or all is well with you,
And God shall hear your words, and make
them true."

Wilcox

4) **fear of**
the loss of love   This fear can also foster that destructive force known as jealousy and will rear its ugly head to certain destruction of success. I'm sure that we have learned much about the disasters of life associated with jealousy or the constant fear of losing a partner to another. The resulting damage of these fears is often represented in movies, books and the media as well as in the real-life examples around us.

5) fear of old age

This is another fear that can certainly be overcome. If we look carefully in all of the history books, science books, etc. we can come to the realization that a large number of the greatest achievements, inventions, and accomplishments have occurred in the lives of great persons who had reached the age of fifty and on into the ages of 65- 75 years of age.

Stay active and fit, read many diverse books, engage in activities that will keep your mind sharp. We see many people out there on the bike paths who are well over the age of sixty and seventy. Spending time with younger people also keeps you in tune and "young". When it comes to mature friendships, age should never be a consideration. My mom is in her seventies and she is my "best friend." She can out shop my daughters and often helps to pick out their clothes. She thinks positively and rarely lets her aches and pains (she has rheumatoid arthritis) keep her at home. A smile is a constant physical characteristic of that ageless face and many comment on how youthful she looks. In her, I see the reason not to fear old age.

6) fear of death

Let's leave that fear until our "death date", shall we? So many people are afraid of dying that they can actually speed up the process by dwelling on it. Understand, as my husband says, "that no one is getting out of here alive" and live with the fact that it is a natural process to be dealt with "when the time comes." Don't waste precious days, months or even years worrying about the inevitable. Live life to the fullest, make each day count and take on the challenges of life as they arrive, when they arrive, and not a moment before.

(3)*"Any dominating idea, plan, or purpose which you hold in your mind through repetition of thought and which is emotionalized with a burning desire for its realization is taken over by the subconscious section of the mind and acted upon through whatever natural and logical means that may be available."*

Napoleon Hill

The "burning desire" here is the key. If you really want it, if you really believe that you can achieve it, you **combine that desire, plan, or purpose with** that state of mind known as

(4) **faith**, it will be taken over by the subconscious of the mind and acted upon almost immediately. You have the power to make anything happen if you have that burning desire which motivates, pushes, and brings about the goal.

First we have to realize our own natural power to do these things;

second, we must sow the seed or idea by actually visualizing it, seeing it in our mind's eye;

third, we must have the **faith** to hold our ideals steady in the face of any possible opposition, fear, or material condition.

(5) The **power of thought** is the only part of a human being that he/she has total control over. It is the one thing that is sufficient for man's need to attain success if it is used properly.

"There isn't anything that you can't achieve which you can conceive and believe." N. Hill

If you can conceive an idea, a plan, or a purpose and believe that you can achieve it, you can find out ways and means of doing it but you have to be definite about it. You have to be specific, you have to know what it is you want, you have to know why you want it, and what you're going to give in return for it.

Nature frowns upon the idea of getting something for nothing and I will be dealing with that issue a little later on in the book, the chapter which is titled, "Going the Extra Mile."

(6) The last interesting thing that Napoleon Hill gives us in this theory is that **"the subconscious section of the mind appears to be the only doorway of an individual's approach to infinite intelligence"**.

Our inner mind, our thoughts, can communicate with that infinite intelligence (whatever it may be for whomever it may be [God, Buddha, the Great One, etc.]) and can gain strength, knowledge, and ultimate wisdom from the higher power that we choose to communicate with.

You may ask the obvious question. "Why has Ingrid Hearn spent an entire chapter reiterating Napoleon Hill's "Steps for Success"?

I believe that, in order for you to be an effective educator, you must become successful. You must carry the aura of success. You must present yourself as a successful individual and you must FEEL successful.

Why?

You are representing the future to your students. You exemplify the person they may wish to emulate and you will definitely be one of those influential people who will help them to achieve their goals. You are the one individual in that classroom who will be directing them in a positive way. Your wish is for them to learn, to become better, to achieve success. If you do not represent yourself as a successful individual, you will have not have the power to successfully teach others. Think of some of the teachers you have had in your life. Remember the successful ones? Of course you do. Remember the ho'hum ones? Probably not. Remember the serious duds? Bingo!

How do you wish to be remembered?

If you want to learn how...you must learn from the best who...

Learn these steps to success, share them with your students in whatever way you can (creativity becomes the key) and you will see successful results in your classroom.

Read carefully, the following definitions taken from the Webster's Dictionary

Success - (1)"a favorable or prosperous course or termination of anything attempted; prosperous or advantageous issue." (2) "a successful person or affair" (3) "the issue or result, favorable or unfavorable"

Successful - (1) "of persons attaining what one desires or intends; especially having reached a high degree of worldly prosperity" (2) "of things, terminating in or meeting with success; resulting favorably: said of a course of action"

Synonyms - auspicious, fortunate, **happy**

Is this something that you have incorporated into your life?

"For the best verse hasn't been rhymed yet,
The best house hasn't been planned
The highest peak hasn't been climbed yet,
The mightiest rivers aren't spanned.
Don't worry and fret, faint hearted
The chances have just begun,
For the Best jobs haven't been started,
The Best work hasn't been done."

Braley

"YOU MUST PERSONIFY THE VERY THING YOU WISH TO TEACH OTHERS TO BECOME".

How can you expect your students to achieve greatness if they do not know what greatness is? Understand that there will be future lawyers, mothers, doctors, fathers, politicians etc. in your classes. What better time to help them find their greatness than in your classroom? Even the youngest of students will discover their true beginnings in you and in your lessons. Make those opportunities count. Give them the best and teach them "success".

13

The Subconscious Mind

"The great were once as you.
They whom men magnify today
Once groped and blundered on life's way,
Were fearful themselves, and thought
By magic was men's greatness wrought.
They feared to try what they could do;
Yet Fame hath crowned with her success
The selfsame gifts that you possess."

Edgar Guest

"We build our fortune thought by thought,
For so the universe was wrought,
Thought is another name for fate:
Choose then the destiny and wait,
For love brings love and hate brings hate."

Van Dyke

"THE LADDER OF SUCCESS IS NEVER CROWDED AT THE TOP"

N. Hill

CHAPTER TWO
WHY ARE YOU HERE?

There are as many reasons for wishing to become a teacher as there are months of the year. A few examples:

1) summers and holidays off

This is my personal favorite because everyone knows that, after spending approximately ten months in a room filled with 30-40 noisy children all day, five days a week, no one could possibly want or need to have a rest. Don't you love those parents who are breaking down the doors in September after having to spend two whole months with their offspring?

2) couldn't pass bar exam

I love this one because it goes with the old saying
"Those who can - do; those who cannot - teach!"
This is one of the great myths of all time. Everyone should know that "if you can't do - you can't teach".
I actually know a man who found this to be a serious truth. He was completing the last month of his student teaching block in Grade One. A little boy put up his hand to be excused. Before this student teacher could even give his permission, a little puddle began to form on the floor.
This man is now a prominent lawyer and has never looked back. Just a little story.

15

3) would like to be the boss
for a change Let me guess.

You were never allowed to be in charge and this is your big chance. Got a chip on your shoulder? Don't take it into the classroom. Children can read you like a book and you will pay.

4) always wanted to be an
authority figure and found
out that four year olds are
intimidated by a deep voice.

This sounds like one of those needy people whose own children don't listen to him and he has a need to have authority over someone's kids.

This could be taken in fun and I hope that it is indeed funny because I have often wondered if the reasons listed here were perhaps the reasons that some of the teachers who taught me during school entered the teaching profession.

"If you don't know where you're going, you're never gonna get there."

Yogi Berra

Let's Get Serious

Taking things a little more seriously, I have interviewed many young people and also those "more mature" people who are changing careers. One of the sections of my questionnaire asks that they look back in their lives to a time where they fondly remember that **one special teacher**, the one who had faith in them.

It is with delight that I witness the change in their persona. Their eyes light up, their faces soften and they begin to share in vivid detail, the adventures they encountered in that special person's class.

Let's look at you. You could have been at a crisis point in your life, realized that you were not cut out to be an academic scholar, or just failed to be motivated. Along came this wonderful, positive "creature teacher" who showed you the good stuff - your potential, your talents and your ability to see things in a different way. He/she tweaked your learning style enough so that you actually "got it". The light bulb went on.

This miracle worker changed the course of your life and here you are, wishing to do the same for another human being.

Good for you!

This is one of the best reasons there are for becoming an educator and it will be the one that will keep you firmly rooted in this profession.

It is important for you to solidify your reason to teach. Write it down, read it often, and don't allow adversities to sway you. You are enthusiastic, energetic, and full of "life-changing" ideas.

Hold fast!

Never lose sight of all of those great reasons that caused you to take this journey. I stress this because you will, at some point, question your abilities, your totally disastrous lessons (you will have at least one), and those art ideas that seemed so creative at the time. Your path will be fraught with criticism and disappointment.

I know that it sounds much like the lyrics of a bad country/western song but this will happen. You will at some point during your career, question your abilities, motives, and even your choice of profession.

If you don't question your choice of profession at some point in your life, you are doing something wrong.

"Every adversity, every failure and every heartache carries with it the Seed of an equivalent or a greater benefit." N. Hill

17

CHAPTER THREE
Can you Handle Criticism?

Criticism is a fact of life and **if you understand that you cannot and will not please everyone**, then prepare yourself accordingly. If we could be the ideal mate for everyone in the world, what a sad world it would be. We, as humans, innately wish to please everyone and, even though this is an admirable quality, it is not an attainable one. Individuals who compromise at every turn soon lose their identity and the ability to achieve true success.

When your principal criticizes you, learn and become better for it. Not every principal will be as kind, loving, and empathetic as ALL OF MINE WERE. (surely, I jest)

They too are human and are in the learning process right alongside of you. Often, their frustrations become your responsibility and, when it becomes too difficult a burden, you may have to make the decision to either accept the burden or move on. It's not necessarily a bad thing to move on. Fate generally pushes you in another direction for the good. I deal with this very issue in Chapter Fourteen.

"ANY EVALUATION IS BASED FROM A PERCEPTION OF TIME AND A FEELING IN TIME."
CHANGE EITHER VARIABLE, AND YOU CHANGE WHAT IS POSSIBLE"

Don Wolfe

I worked with an amazing teacher who truly loves her students and the teaching profession. She had experienced a very disheartening challenge with her last principal who had gone to great lengths to make her feel very ineffective and unworthy as a teacher. It became an unbearable situation and she applied for a transfer. It was granted shortly after the request was made; without meeting or consultation.

Upon her arrival at our June meeting, we learned that she had no prior knowledge of our school and was quite bitter about her new placement. Her self-esteem had been injured and her talent for teaching questioned.

After a couple of weeks into September, she came to the realization that our school was exactly where she belonged. The principal was very appreciative of her efforts. She consulted with her on a regular basis and assisted her in working out any difficulties she may have had. Our entire staff made no secret of how they felt about this woman's "way with children" and supported her at every turn. It was a pleasure and a joy to work at this school because of the peer support system in place. Together we lifted each other up.

I am happy to say that, while I write, she is still teaching at this school and feels that it has proven to be the best placement for her, even though she had not made the choice herself. I love and respect twists of fate.

Does she feel that her teaching has improved? She openly discusses with others who may be struggling, that this adversity has strengthened her and ultimately made her a better teacher. She could have accepted defeat, perhaps even quit her job. It would have been disastrous and many children would be missing out on the incredible, exciting experiences that this loving teacher provides on a daily basis.

Adversities and challenges are a part of life. I've seen these simply stated bumper stickers all over the country "Shit happens." Can't be much clearer than that!

If we see each difficulty as a learning experience and work through it as this teacher did, the compilation of these experiences can become our best opportunities for growth.

Does it feel good at the time? No way! Can you turn it into a great situation? There is a way!

"LEARN TO LOVE YOURSELF - EVEN WHEN YOU DON'T"
Don Wolfe

19

Do we build stumbling blocks or stepping stones?

"Isn't is strange that princes and kings
And clowns that cavort in sawdust rings,
And common folk like you and me
Are all builders for eternity?

To each is given a book of rules
A block of stone; a bag of tools,
And each must build before time has flown
A stumbling block or a stepping stone."

If we have learned to build stepping stones rather than stumbling blocks in our own lives, just think of how meaningful our lessons become as we teach children to do the same. Providing this insight during their early years is a powerful tool that can influence them in the most positive way.

"If we can touch one - even one; our job is done."

There is a catchy phrase that one of my students used to quote when he was faced with a challenge. It is taken from some popular movie and I think it is very fitting. I have borrowed it and use it from time to time.

"I laugh at the face of adversity".

Can we laugh at the face of adversity? Can we learn to turn it around?

We must learn to practice this motto in our own lives and then share it effectively with our students. Children who are able to handle the difficult situations of each stage of growth will be much more equipped to tackle life's challenges as they appear. It is a step by step lesson beginning with baby steps and developing into the giant steps of their future.

"By perseverance, the snail reached the ark."

Charles Haddon Spurgeon

"ADVICE"

"A kind, constructive suggestion now and then from people around you should not be received with resentment, but alas! How few of us can bear to think our actions are being criticized. Somehow, each of us seems to have the subconscious feeling that really, if we have not intended any wrong, what we do is never out of order.

Everyone is human - we all like to believe that we're right and indispensable to the world around us. Consequently, in many instances, we are pretty free with the advice that we frequently hand out.

If you seem to be on the receiving end of suggestions most of the time, perhaps you should take account of your speech and action, and stop, look and listen. After all, it could be you instead of the other fellow."

Joanne D'Alton Clancy
"A way out from in"

"GET TO THE HEART OF THE MATTER AND YOU CAN CHANGE WHAT IS THE MATTER."

Don Wolfe

TAKE A STEP BACK

Look back in your own life to a time of adversity or hardship. Think seriously about your reaction and your ability to cope with the problem.

Were you afraid or unsure?

Did you know that, ultimately, it would be resolved?

Would you have benefited from the realization that it was a challenge or life-test that could make you stronger or did you already have that benefit?

How did you handle it?

What was the result?

Is it now a memory?

Does it seem as big a problem now as it did then?

Did you get over it and move on?

During each period of our lives, we hit stumbling blocks. **They are inevitable** and they teach us many things. Use them as learning tools. They are free! No tuition fees.

21

If we follow and study the timeless stories and detailed accounts of many great leaders throughout history, we are privy to the obvious lesson that no one escapes the "blocks of stone" obstructing life's path. They are the "stepping stones" for the courageous and successful individuals of the world. Welcome!

AN EXAMPLE

"He went into the Black Hawk War as a Captain and came out as a Private; he lost his first business; then he ran for state legislature and lost; he was said to have suffered a nervous breakdown; he ran for Congress and lost, later elected, his re-election campaign was defeated; he ran for the Senate and lost; he tried for the Vice-Presidential nomination and lost; he ran for the Senate again and lost — Then he became the 16th President of the United States of America."

This man was **Abraham Lincoln.** I'd say that there were a few stumbling blocks in this man's life.

This is just one of the many stories of famous, successful people who would not allow the stumbling blocks of life to obstruct their vision. Instead, they used their negative experiences to build a strong pathway to the future they envisioned for themselves.

I'm sure that if you look at some of the difficulties that your friends, family or even you, yourself, have already had to overcome in life, you will find examples of this very thing on your own doorstep. It's all in how you deal with it. **Don't allow yourself to become a victim!**

Take the opportunities that Nature has given you to build a better and stronger path for your life. My friends and family are my courageous role models. They have faced the "stumbling blocks" of life and have dealt with them in a positive way. Their examples have helped me to face my challenges and together, we have been able to create "stepping stones" for our success.

Build a positive force around you, stay strong by surrounding yourself with people who share these strengthening philosophies and practice them in their own lives and use life's stumbling blocks to build solid stepping stones for your future and for the future of those around you.

"A mirror reflects a man's face, but what he is really like is shown by the kind of friends he chooses."

The Living Bible Proverbs 28

As I was reading the very thought-provoking book, "You Inc." written by **Burke Hedges**, I came across an interesting section on positive thinking. I would like to relate it to you.

I CAN vs. I CAN'T

Have you noticed that there is a lot more I CAN'T thinking going on in children than I CAN! There is an interesting story taken from the book "Teacher Talk" by Chick Moorman. The story concerns a fourth grade teacher named Donna who devised a creative way for her students to stop thinking in the I CAN'T mode and begin to think in terms of I CAN.

Early in the year, Donna asked her class of 31 students to take out a clean sheet of paper and write the words "I CAN'T" in big capital letters at the top of the page. She then asked them to write a list of all of the things that they couldn't do. Some of them wrote:

"I can't pass a math test."

"I can't do 10 push-ups."

"I can't get Debbie to like me."

While the students were busily writing their lists, Donna wrote a list of her own.

"I can't get Johny's mother to come in for an interview."

"I can't get Alan to use his words instead of his fists."

THE FUNERAL - CONTINUES

When the lists were completed, Donna asked the children to fold their papers in half and drop them into an empty shoe box on her desk. Once the papers were collected, Donna put the lid on the box, tucked it under her arm, and instructed the students to follow her out the door and onto the playground.

She marched them to the outskirts of the yard. Turning toward them with a solemn expression she announced, "Children, we are gathered here today for a very serious occasion. We are going to bury, I CAN'T."

She then proceeded to dig a hole in the ground. The digging took quite a few minutes because each child wanted to have a turn. By the time each child had dug out a shovel full of dirt, the hole was three feet deep. Donna gently placed the box of papers into the bottom of the freshly dug grave.

Then she turned to her students and asked them to form a circle around the grave, join hands, and bow their heads. Here is the unforgettable eulogy that she gave.

"Friends, we gather today to honor the memory of I CAN'T. While he was with us on earth, he touched the lives of everyone...some, more than others. His name, unfortunately, has been spoken in every public building - schools, city halls, state capitals, and, yes, even our White House.

"Today, we have provided I CAN'T with a final resting place. He is survived by his brothers and sisters - I CAN...I WILL... and I'M GOING RIGHT AWAY. They are not as well known as their famous relative...and are not as strong and powerful yet. Perhaps someday, with your help, they will make an even bigger mark on the world.

"May I CAN'T rest in peace...and may everyone present pick up their lives and move forward in his absence. Amen."

Then Donna and her students filled in the fresh grave before returning to the classroom, where they celebrated the passing of I CAN'T. As part of the celebration, Donna cut out a large tombstone from butcher paper and wrote in big, black letters these words:

I CAN'T
MAY HE REST IN PEACE
MARCH 28, 1980

This paper tombstone hung in Donna's classroom for the rest of the year. Whenever one of her students forgot and said, "I can't" Donna would point to the tombstone. More often than not, the student would smile and rephrase the statement.

My Grade 8 class decided to cremate "I CAN'T" in our ceremony and our tombstone was cut from a large sheet of grey bristleboard. It took its prominent place on the front bulletin board along with other "memorable moments". As rotary children entered, they would see it and ask questions. My students couldn't wait to explain what it was all about.

I enjoyed this story and I enjoyed the ceremony even more. Try it...you'll like it. Thank you Mr. Hedges for your many inspirational stories. My students have enjoyed many of your fine examples of success stories.

"LEARN TO EITHER GET WHAT YOU WANT...OR WANT WHAT YOU ARE GETTING."
Don Wolfe

CHAPTER FOUR

What is Your Job?

I pledge allegiance
To the children of the world
And to the earth on which we stand.

One people, whose differences we respect;
One earth we promise to protect;
One goal, to live in love and peace.

Harold W. Peterson

You may think that this poem is a little "out there" but that's because you are an adult. Children need to live in this world. They need to believe in this poem at the outset of their journey through life. Things will get tough enough; soon enough, and they need to hold on to the solid values that you, their teacher, will help to instill in abundance during your time together.

Your job or role as a teacher is to take your students from the state of knowing less (referred to as the elementary state) to the state of knowing more.

You must teach children the strategies to enable them to learn for themselves in order for them to learn more. By using repetition and modeling, students will learn and enter a state of knowing more. They can't help it! By going through the following stages in various ways and with many mediums, their learning style will be targeted somewhere in there. (Chapter thirteen delves into the various learning styles in more detail)

The path is the journey and it should be filled with not only information but adventure, wonder, awe, personal growth and a lot of fun. During these stages, remember to maintain a positive outlook and stay as enthusiastic as possible. If you do this, I promise you, that you will enjoy the process so much more, but most importantly, so will your students.

"LEARN TO LOVE
AND
LOVE TO LEARN"
A Don Wolfe Winspiration

A NO-FAIL RECIPE FOR TEACHING CHILDREN

According to my research, there are **4 main stages** in the Process of Learning.

(1) Elementary. This is the beginning, the introduction. What are we learning about?

(2) Informational. This is the acquisition of the information needed to learn about the subject; in other words, the learning of information.

(3) Analytical. This is where students analyze the knowledge that they have acquired from the various sources of research. It must be checked out and reviewed from all angles. Often debates can be slotted into this category.

(4) Summation. All of the information is put together and sense is made of all the components.

You must follow this process to achieve successful learning. It can be done very quickly or over a period of time, depending upon the material and topics being studied. If you follow this model through these stages, successful learning will take place. This is the pattern. Your job is to take the pattern and use it creatively every time you teach a new concept. The creativity comes into play in numbers 2,3 and 4.

I realize that the word RUBRIC has been used at nauseam but it is a very useful tool. The mystifying rubrics that the ordinary person cannot pronounce or understand will become clear and second nature to you as you wield them with knowledge and power. They give children a clearly written chart of instructions to follow. Many times, I invite the class to join me in creating a rubric. It gives them ownership and more motivation to follow the standards set. Some of the "wonderful" headings that we have come up with are:

(1)"Bogus", (2)"Getting there",(3)"Acceptable",(4) "Awesome" - Grades 7/8 example

(1) "Yucky" (2)"Less Yucky", (3)"Okay", (4)"Cool" - Grades 4/5 example

27

These four titles represent the four levels that are identified by the present Course Curriculum Guides.

Level 1 (not acceptable for a passing grade)

Level 2 (barely acceptable, but a passing grade)

Level 3 (an average level where most of the criteria are met)

Level 4 (the ultimate level where students reach the full criteria of the assignment and succeed).

Students get a big kick out of following their own directions and I have actually experienced better results in much of their work. One of the beauties of creating the rubric as a class is that it allows you to fully discuss the project in great detail without the students getting bored or annoyed. They participate in creating appropriate standards and actually explain their own detailed expectations of the assignment. They set higher standards for themselves by virtue of their own choices.

Your charted rubric can deal with whatever you wish, ranging from the use of typed or written print to the description of illustrations. All generalization is gone and no student can use the excuse that "they didn't know".

I realize that these titles, used as examples for the rubrics, sound a little less than professional but let's look at its ultimate purpose. Is it being met?

An interesting writing assignment is for students to take ownership of creating individual rubrics for their writing portfolio. They love to set their own standards and rise to the challenge of meeting them.

Let's Break it all Down

(1) The **Elementary stage** of this process is provided for you.

It comes in the form of the current curriculum documents; the most modern curriculum guide set by the government in charge. Over the years, these guides have taken on many different forms but their content is generally the same. Although curriculum documents are overloaded, the true realization is: How much can they change grammar, mathematics, and social studies? The key is not to allow the overwhelming content to control you but instead, take ownership of it, and accept the challenge of "playing with it" to make it fun and interesting. It becomes your mission, should you wish to accept it, and becomes the focal point of "the game". Too often, teachers complain about the Curriculum Guides at nauseam. Understand this fact: **curriculum guides are not going to disappear** and the energy that one uses to complain about them could be used to constructively develop lesson plans to teach what is in them.

(2) **Informational learning** should come from a wide variety of sources. Students should be spending equal time researching books, pamphlets, brochures, and magazines as well as the Internet, computer programs, each other, and members of family and community. Too many teachers feel pressured to push computers as the new, more effective way to research. Often valuable books are left by the wayside. Balance is the key!

Do not underestimate the power of a good index in a resource book. It allows for ease and speed in finding information. Often, the Internet creates problems by using allotted time ineffectively. When using the research engines of the Internet, teach younger, more inexperienced students as a group! Guide them through each step as a class to avoid unnecessary rambling and surfing. (or veering off into an unacceptable web site)

Introduce students to a unit, topic, project... by **brainstorming**. In order for students to create, they should understand that everything you create *"begins as an offspring of something that has already been done. The thing that you create must be developed from materials that are available."* Howard Hill - "Energizing the 12 Powers of Your Mind"

When they take all of the information to the last stage of culmination, they will come to realize the truthfulness of this statement.

Teach or review point form notes early in the year in order for students to thoroughly understand the information being researched. In order to make a point form note IN THEIR OWN WORDS, they must read and be able to understand what is being read. **It is important for children of all ages to learn how to make point form notes.** It develops their thought processes and allows them to rethink and rewrite information.

29

Informational learning can become entertaining when students collect data for surveys. It becomes challenging when children are left to their own devices in finding ways of gleaning information. Spend as much time as you see fit in order to teach the process of creating successful point form notes. This is a very necessary skill that they will utilize at all levels of education. It builds their own independent material without the threat of plagerism.

Even when using the Internet and printing off information, I have students make point form notes from the information that they have collected.

Highlighting is a good practice, but it cannot replace the thoughts that go into rewriting and compacting information. It is the process that is important, not only the written results.

I evaluate point form notes as well as completed work.

(3) **Analyzing** can become an extremely interesting and thought-provoking stage in the process of learning.

Make this fun! (I will deal with the topic of "fun in the classroom" a little later on). Build webs on the board, create debates by choosing teams to support and dispute topics, have students critique the research of other students, appoint peer tutors or assign partners to expand upon and edit information.

Most students love to share their knowledge and experiences. Wonderful class discussions can erupt at any moment when you are analyzing the topics being studied. This is the fun-filled section of learning and should be a motivating, delightful experience. Encourage students to come up with their own ideas to add to your methods of analyzing.

If you have difficulty incorporating drama into your program, here is your chance! Short skits providing ideas, opinions, and results of surveys are an interesting and delightful way for children to lose their inhibitions in front of their peers while analyzing the researched work.

(4) **Summation.** This is the culmination of all learned materials. There are so many ways to present learned information that I hardly know where to begin.

With pens and paper flying, information can be presented on bristle board or cardboard, orally in front of the class or on tape, visually with the use of a cam corder or slides. It can be acted out and written about. It can be artistic and colorful or methodically black and white. The sky's the limit and you are the designer of this section.

I had a delightful experience in my Grade 4/5 class when delving into a "Mystery Unit." Alien beings soon entered the conversation and excited children contributed animated explanations and interpretations of "what aliens are". From there, we moved on to "mysterious and unusual life forms" deciding to create some of our own. Even the parents got involved in the mind-bending endeavors.

These "monster pets", ranging from one inch in diameter to four feet in height, came to life as enthusiastic, artistic children molded and shaped them from clay, papier mache, plastic bottles, plasticine, pop cans, coat hangers, pipe cleaners, string, rope and other exotic art materials.

Their creatures sported unusual eating habits, survived in unconventional environments (one lived in the child's freezer), and boasted of a seemingly logical history and place of origin.

Their environments were established around them and the entire effort landed safely on display tables running down the full length of the junior hallway. Brightly colored posters provided explicit and "factual" information to the many passers by and maternal children stood proudly to guard and explain all of the details surrounding the life of their fascinating "babies".

It was a very successful culmination of many reading, writing and oral language skills outlined in the curriculum guide.

Again, be the creative genius that you are!

Consciousness

It is important to realize what the word "consciousness" means. Even though, you may know something to be true, it is still not necessarily part of your consciousness.

Mathematics (as you will realize more and more) has never been my strength. I have worked hard to try and overcome the truth of that statement and to make the components of mathematics more a part of my consciousness.

During a few of my Grade 8 teaching years, I was assigned to teach the subject of Mathematics. My students would sit patiently as I would work out a problem on the blackboard. They understood that it could be done, they watched me go through the steps and they agreed that the outcome was the correct answer. The difficulty became evident when the next question was presented to them and they had to "work it out". Even though they had watched me complete the first one on the board in front of them with their input, the process of solving it was not clearly evident to many.

As a class, we would work on approximately 10 of these questions together on the board. I invited students to come up and explain the steps as they solved the problem. Slowly, as the class answered the "yes and no" questions that I asked continuously during the exercise, we made the entire process of solving these questions a part of our consciousness.

Did every student now understand how to solve the problems? No.
Did many of the students understand the process? Yes.

We then proceeded to create a pattern, a table of questions if you will, which caused class brainstorming and even more light bulbs to go on.

Discussion and clarity of steps brought about more understanding and, at the end of the unit, a very high success rate was achieved during evaluation. Even though the students had been able to intellectually perceive the solution of the problems at the beginning, they had to guide those lessons into their consciousness, making them a part of their own thought process.

In the chapter Teaching through Learning Channels, you will receive many ideas and ways in which to help children put more information into their consciousness.

From here, I would like to extend the journey to the two approaches to learning. If we wish to teach successfully, we must teach children to learn successfully.

TWO APPROACHES TO LEARNING
THE LEARNING GAME

I have taken this list directly from the WINKIDS manual written by Robert Allen and Donald S. Wolfe. It is a very powerful list and provides a much clearer perspective of learning habits.

Children can become informed or transformed in your classroom.

INFORMATIONAL	TRANSFORMATIONAL
structured	creative
what you learn	how you learn
effort	ease
objective/logical	personal/emotional
what's known/history	what's new/discovery
serious/real	curious/play
same/automatic	different/spontaneous
repetition	intuition
passive involvement	massive involvement
hold back/protect	let go/trust
competition/being the best	cooperation/being your best
answer from outside	answer from within
alone	all one
right/wrong	all right
uh oh!	Aha!

While the informational learning column has obvious important uses, the right column creates the real differences in motivation, attitude and most importantly amazing results.

Imagination

"Imagination rules the World"

Napoleon Bonaparte

The word "imagination" should always be associated with the word **"learning"**. Children who can come up with new ideas usually possesses an unusual combination of imagination and a persistent refusal to conform to the regular way of doing things. They often avoid routine ways of completing their assignments.

"Imagination is making new wholes out of familiar parts."

Howard E. Hill

Although day dreaming is an integral part of creating, children must be taught to curb it at some point. There is a need to clarify their purpose and the direction in which to focus their dreams or thoughts.

Aimless daydreaming is neither practical nor productive. When a goal and direction are added, something has to happen. There must be movement in order for the task to be accomplished.

CHAPTER FIVE
YOU CAN MAKE IT IF YOU TRY

Now that we have completed a fairly thorough study of how we process information, we need to look at the actual information itself. Yes, there is a huge amount of it! **Overwhelming, isn't it?** The good news is that it doesn't have to be. Let's look at that statement carefully. **It doesn't have to be overwhelming!**

As an educator, you have the option of putting the elementary information (the objectives outlined in the curriculum) into your order of importance.

You make the decision of whether it should be taught as an in-depth unit or it should be touched upon lightly.

Does each topic require equal time?

Do we review at nauseam?

Do we teach to tests?

So many questions-so little time.

The one thing that I learned a long time ago was that sometimes, if I put the actual questions of a test on the board the day before the test, my students would go home and study those questions in order to complete them successfully. **Did I cheat?** OR Did I get them to accomplish exactly what I wanted?

Good question but the answer is obvious. If you want your class to learn a specific group of facts, give them the questions ahead of time. They will be focused and they will study the answers to those questions. Why fog their minds with things that are unnecessary? I often test to teach rather than teach to tests. The results are better grades, a higher level of self-esteem and a greater overall percentage of success. Obviously, I do not practice this method all of the time, but it has its place as a very successful teaching tool in drilling particular points of importance.

What is it that we are actually trying to instill in our students? The ability to learn and increase their knowledge of facts is important but, parented with that, should be the knowledge that they can and will, in fact, achieve success! It is important for us to provide opportunities for each and every one in our classroom to feel this success. Getting back to the huge amount of information.

How many subjects do you teach?

This is a very important question when it comes to integrating subject matter. If you have a homeroom and teach English language, grammar, reading, writing, history, geography, and mathematics, you have much more leeway with integrating than the person teaching one subject area. If you teach only one or two subjects, the need to cover huge amounts of information in many areas is not as overwhelming for you and so again, there is some balance. The next section of this chapter addresses the needs of the teacher who is faced with a variety of subject areas and a deluge of information to be taught.

Blending

Let me explain, with an example, how you can easily and, more importantly, in a fun and interesting way, blend two subject areas effectively.

Example

History -War of 1812	**Music**
-famous people	-teaching styles of music
-reasons for the war	-rap style which is modern, speaking style
-reactions of both sides	-take pertinent information from war
-war itself	-create a rap song to condense the war
-outcomes of the war	-perform for the class

Just as the "Wreck of the Edmund Fitzgerald" was a song written by a history teacher to explain the events of that tragedy, we too can parrot this idea to teach our lessons more effectively.

Take your history program into your music class and "kill the proverbial two birds with one stone".

One step further takes it into the English writing class where a group of students work together to "collaborate" and voila, you have major integration targeting at least three or four items in the course outline. You now evaluate accordingly. English, music, and history marks can be gleaned from this assignment. What new teachers often do not realize is that you may teach writing skills in geography class and compile marks for both English and geography.

It becomes a very useful and interesting exercise to study each subject area closely and look at what you can mix and match. It's like a puzzle or a game if you will, and teachers, as a rule, innately love puzzles so this should be right up your alley.

I say that teachers like puzzles rather than games because I still don't attend wedding or baby showers on time for fear of having to attach clothespins to my silk shirt or unscramble fifty words on a designated piece of paper in a limited number of minutes. I like to think of teachers as people who appreciate more refined and useful games than choosing a beautifully wrapped gift from a pile and then having to give it up to some crazed woman in the group who derives great pleasure in snatching it away from you because her number was been picked after yours. I have always believed that if you were picked as the first or "winning" number, you should get the prize but in this game, if you are the first winner chosen, you are a LOSER! I would know that because, for the first time in my life, I was picked at the very beginning and actually believed that I was a WINNER! I have gone through the process that teaches me that I am a winner anyway, (Chapter 22) so now it doesn't matter any more and, besides, my daughter Rebecca, gave me her present to make me feel better.

Men will be puzzled by these examples but any woman worth her salt has participated in at least one of these notorious "fun" activities at a female celebration. I don't get it but I guess it's supposed to be fun so I have been caught with clothespins on my pants when I miscalculated the "game time". I'm sure there is a male equivalent to this ritual but I haven't found out what it is yet and I'm not sure that I really want to know. Again, I digress. Back to "The Game".

The Wardrobe Game

Ladies, we do this with our wardrobe each season. How many times have you asked yourself, "what can I wear with these shoes; this skirt; this sweater?"

It can be a lot of fun as well as challenging when you are on a limited budget and wish to be creative.

Years ago, when I was a financially-challenged student at Brock University, I had a part-time position teaching piano on the upper floor of a local studio. Grand pianos were being sold by professionals in the retail showroom below and I was encouraged to dress appropriately in order to be part of the "team". With my minimal income and maximum bills, I faced a serious dilemma.

Upon scouting the neighborhood, I discovered a Christian Benefit Shop which sold, among other things, a wide variety of clothing.

A woman with obvious expensive taste had made it a habit to donate her pricey cast-offs on a regular basis. They were just my size and didn't seem to appeal to the women living in that less affluent area of the city. For very little money, I was able to afford beautiful clothes for work and special occasions. With much gratitude for this little miracle in my life, I became a bi-weekly shopper. The fact that I was supporting a charitable organization was a bonus!

I would spend hours laying the various articles out on the bed to see how I could create new outfits from the pieces that I had purchased. (This was my early training in mixing and matching.)

I used the same principle when it came to coordinating subject materials at school. I discovered that it can be just as much fun and challenging to take the skills and information that you have to teach in various subject areas and mix them with each other. Spread things out and make it all come together like a puzzle. Just like I looked pretty "hot" way back then, your program can get pretty "hot" and exciting.

Anyway, getting back to mixing and matching- get the idea? I know that men would never admit to doing what I just explained so we'll leave you to your own creative juices. I'm sure that you mix and match in that whole football, baseball betting pool thing that I have participated and even won money in, but to this day have never understood.

"TRYING"

"How long should a person keep trying to achieve a set goal? And who is to decide whether that goal is out of all realm of possibility?
If, after heartbreaking effort and being rebuffed time and time again, you can still face and evaluate your disappointment, yet have the courage to keep on trying - then your objective may still be in reach, but by an entirely different method.
Don't ever give up trying even if you are kept wondering whether you will ever accomplish what you set out to do. Just remember - present always is the intangible Agent "Who moves in mysterious ways His wonders to perform."

Joanne D'Alton Clancy

Remember - "Triumph Begins With Try"

CHAPTER SIX

HABITS

"Men do not decide their future. They decide their HABITS...and their habits decide their future."

Anonymous

Definition:

A habit is "an acquired pattern of action that is so automatic, it is difficult to break."

Burke Hedges relates in his book "You, Inc."

"People who acquire productive habits are far more likely to be successful...and fulfilled...and in control...than people who acquire unproductive habits."

Steven Covey was the first person to point out the awesome power of effective habits and to communicate the idea that effective habits can be learned and taught to others. He puts this message out in his best-selling book **"Seven Habits of Highly Effective People."**

This routine or pattern of learning brings me to a very important section of the book. I base much of this information found on the book "Key to Yourself" written by a woman named Venice Bloodworth, published by SCRIVENER & COMPANY in 1977.

I would like to take credit for these ideas but it is not mine to take. I have learned much from these wonderful authors who address our minds and perceptions in great detail. As I could not express it in a better way, I have quoted much of her chapter on "Habits".

"God gave all men all earth to love,
But since our hearts are small
Ordained for each one spot should prove
Beloved over all;
That is, as He watched Creation's birth,
So we, in godlike mood,
May of our love create our earth
And see that it is good."

-Kipling

"We are creatures of habit in mind and body. Our lives, our physical conditions, our environment, show unerringly what we habitually think."

Venice Bloodworth

Someone once said: "Sow a thought and reap an action; sow an action and reap a habit; sow a habit and reap a character; sow a character and reap a destiny."

"START WHERE YOU ARE IN ORDER TO GET BETTER"
Winspiration

Much of our career depends upon the habits that we live and those that we teach. Again, let me impress upon you that children learn from repetition and modeling.

We have a huge responsibility to model correct principles and behaviors for our students The famous cliche; "do as I say, not as I do" cannot and should not apply to teaching as it has the power to nullify any great life lesson. (and goodness knows that we teach those on a daily basis) We teachers have a much better cliche. "Do as I do and learn from what I say."

Throughout time we have been introduced to many great people who have achieved their success through the practice of a good habit. Instilled early in life, this practice will create a more successful generation for the future. Please read the following Maxim carefully, think about and realize its truth.

Be careful of your thoughts, for your thoughts become words.
Be careful of your words, for your words become actions.
Be careful of your actions, for your actions become habits.
Be careful of your habits, for your habits become your character.
Be careful of your character, for your character becomes your destiny.

Anonymous

If we are going to create a rut - we must choose carefully the type of rut we wish to make a part of our lives.

If you have subjected yourself to a "bad" habit, recognize it and find a way to **replace** it with a good one. This is preferred over trying to break a bad habit as that becomes a much more difficult task.

Self-control is a good habit

It is important for us to learn and teach that we cannot prevent unpleasant things from happening but "WE CAN DEVELOP THE HABIT OF SELF CONTROL AND REALIZE THAT WHAT HAPPENS DOES NOT MATTER BUT YOUR REACTION TO IT IS WHAT COUNTS." Learning to overcome adversities and misfortunes by using positive behaviors and reactions will allow us to one day look back on them as learning opportunities. I must admit there have been many times throughout my career that I have felt the need to quit teaching.

I have felt more than too many times that I was not strong enough to lead children into their future;
- that I had made a huge error in judgement;
- that I was terribly wrong when I reacted physically to a student's outburst;
- that I should never have yelled uncontrollably at a group of children;
- that swearing out loud on a playground was not acceptable;
- that I could not handle the bullying of a child without losing my temper;
- that I did not keep my promise even though I had every intention of doing so;
- that I could not survive the loss of one of my most academic, quick-witted, athletic, loving students to that horrible illness, leukemia.

Yes! I have asked these questions and more. I have not been the perfect example nor have I been the perfect teacher BUT I have learned, oh, I have learned - that through each and every one of these trials, I have become better AND I have become stronger.

It is important to learn to control your emotions, or they will control you. No one can "make" you sad or mad, happy or glad. You choose these emotions. Managing them means understanding that you can't always control what happens to you...but you can control your emotional response to the events around you.

I have learned that I am a mere human who makes mistakes. I have been humbled to the point of humiliation by an angry, yet truthful parent in the staff room and have admitted a secret weakness to a compassionate classroom full of children. Each time, I came to the realization that, no matter what, **I still love and wish to teach children**. They, in return, are loving, forgiving, and embracing creatures who wish to share life's learning **with** you if you are willing to learn **with** them, **admit to mistakes** in front of them and teach them **how to learn from each error**.

Teaching children how to manage their emotions is a huge part of your responsibility as their role model.

A continuous self-talk goes on in my head; "I am striving to become better, and, for the rest of my life, **I will learn to overcome adversity no matter how challenging** it becomes because **I WANT TO CREATE THAT HABIT. I WANT TO BE A SUCCESSFUL TEACHER**." You must talk this out to yourself, remind yourself of your goal, believe it to be true and it will come about. I told you earlier that, once you are a teacher, you will always be a teacher. For me, that is a truth! The students change, but the fact remains.

My ultimate challenge over the last few years has been to create a desire in my students to build good habits for themselves. We have had many class discussions on the topic of good and bad habits. Students have made extensive lists along with the outcomes of each. We have debated many issues surrounding the results of habits, good and bad. We have discussed drinking and drugs as self-destructive habits and compared them to the constructive habits of assigning designated drivers and taking total control of our lives by abstaining from drugs.

Students are always eager to share their own examples of the behaviors being discussed. Even though the topic of creating good habits is not outlined in the Course Curriculum, it becomes the implied responsibility of the teacher. **It is an unwritten rule that we teach good ethics, morals, and habits**. These should be scattered throughout all of our daily lesson plans and inserted whenever the opportunity arises.

They can develop into full blown discussions or merely be touched upon to make a point. Whenever there is a need to pursue an area in more detail, create a designated time period and give it your full attention. Teachers are the masters of their timetables and can "change on a dime", kind of like Superman. Never let the "regular" curriculum work take precedent over an opportunity to teach personal growth to your students.

"It doesn't have to be a long time, it has to be an effective time."

GOOD HABITS SHOULD BE A GOAL FOR ALL

The following is a list of good habits that have been used in my classroom. I'm sure that you can come up with your own as well. I have taken the liberty of listing these in order for you to have concrete, proven examples but please, by no means, accept this as being the best or only list.

Each component becomes the personality of the teacher in charge. Depending upon the age of your students, you may wish to begin with one or two very basic good habits and stretch them into more challenging ones as the years accumulate.

If you happen to be a rotary teacher (as I was for some years), you could begin your lessons with the junior students and continue them all the way to their senior year. The building of good habits is then a cumulative effort and becomes a natural learning process for your students.

I began teaching Grade 4 music and instilled some of my "good habit" goals to these students. Each year, up until Grade 8, the list grew and culminated in my Grade 8 homeroom class. In the junior years, it was more of an oral direction resulting in proficient assignments and positive attitudes towards others. As it grew into the senior years, the list became more detailed and more of an actual written journal for students to use as they furthered their education. The list included short-term and long-term goals which coincide with the forms being used for the transition into secondary school.

Let the list begin!

(1) Get over your anger quickly

Anger is a wasteful emotion and makes you less able to deal with a situation, no matter what it may be. Discussions regarding anger and it's destructive power are an excellent way for children to vent and come to this realization. Ask the question: Who is the most hurt by your being angry? Obviously, the answer is You! "Sometimes, others don't even realize that you are angry and are not affected by it at all and sometimes, your anger causes you to miss out on playing with your friends, missing out on an important event..." This lesson goes right to the top of the school ladder.

As a class, we practiced getting over anger on a regular basis with an exercise to help us switch out of negative emotions. I had the CD player ready with a modern piece of music. I gave the class the emotion "sad" and had them walk around the room in a very sad way while I played about thirty seconds of the music. I stopped the music and gave them the emotion "elated" beginning the music again and watching a classroom of children switch from sadness to extreme happiness in the blink of an eye. (A fun thing to do is to tape little excerpts of music to coincide with the emotions that you will announce. It is a very effective way for children to realize how quickly they can become enveloped by that emotion.)

As they hopped, skipped and jumped in an elated fashion, I would stop the music and yell "angry". Once again, they switched to the new emotion, moving around the room in an angry way for thirty seconds until I yelled "disgusted" and so on... You can use many different emotions for this exercise as well as teaching many adjectives representing the different emotions out there. (**building vocabulary is a major goal of mine and I use every opportunity I can to teach new words**) Students began to realize how quickly they could switch emotions on and off at will and began to practice this in situations out of the classroom, often reporting their results.

Now, the trick is to effectively adapt this ability to real-life situations. This is where drama comes in and the teacher can use "playground dynamics", rejection from a club or sport or various other anger-causing events to "play out" appropriate reactions. You can have a lot of fun with this "good habit training" while teaching very valuable skills in learning how to control anger. The longer you teach this concept, the more you will realize how important this "good" habit is. It is actually one of the more important ones to practice and incorporate into your own life. In my experience, children begin the slow, steady process of replacing destructive thoughts with constructive ones and they tend to get along better.

(2) **Learn from your mistakes**

We all "fall from grace". Don't spend a lot of time "beating yourself up." Shake yourself off, forgive yourself, ask for the forgiveness of those you may have hurt in the process and strive not to repeat that mistake again. I am talking about the hurtful things that have been done or even seemingly harmless acts that were not meant to cause a serious problem.

I ask students to compile a list of "not so nice" things that they feel they have been a part of over the years and how they intentionally or non-intentionally may have hurt others. Bullying is always a concern and we discuss that first. The list is theirs, not to be shared or seen by anyone else. By actually writing a list, they produce a visual, thought-provoking reminder to help them realize the hurt they may have caused. (I make a list as well and find that there are always things on it that I would honestly like to rectify. It's a never-ending process.)

It's always amazing to me how truthful and sincere children can become when they discuss a topic such as this. I love the kind of honesty that emerges and it allows me to see "my" children in a different light. I also find that some of the unknown difficulties that kids deal with lurk in the shadows of these conversations and often find their way to the surface.

During these heartfelt discussions, true learners become more aware of the difficult issues that others may be facing and make the effort to prevent them from getting hurt in the future. One year, we built a fire in a huge garbage can and actually burned our lists of past mistakes, vowing to make a serious effort never to repeat those errors again.

A Meaningful Example

It came out in one of our many class discussions that the "other" kids were being mean to Ben, one of the new boys in the class. He lived on a farm on the outskirts of town and was being teased about being a farm boy with "too short pants". Some of the questions being asked were,

"Why can't his parents just buy him new pants that fit?" and "Doesn't his mother have style?"

The children in the other classes were merciless and couldn't stay away from Ben. They had a need to poke fun and, even though his classmates said that they had tried to defend him, many eventually admitted to having joined the others in taunting him. "They couldn't help it."

It was at this point that great bubble-like tears began to stream down Ben's face and I realized that things had gone further than I had anticipated. I explained to this newcomer that this would be a good opportunity to express to his fellow classmates just how he felt about being teased. He looked up at me with such pain-filled eyes that I could hardly believe he was only nine years of age. Slowly, he began to explain that it didn't bother him at all that his pants were too short and he could even handle the teasing of the children.

He understood that there was a problem with his pants. What bothered him was that his grandmother might find out that he was being poked fun of and feel obligated to buy him new clothes.

"She can't afford it," he sobbed, "and I already caused her enough trouble 'cause she had to sell her house and move here when my mom and dad died."

In his view, his grandmother, who had been taking care of him since his parents were killed in a car accident the year before, had enough things to worry about. He didn't want to ask for new clothes because he already felt that he cost her a lot of money. He was far more upset about being a burden to her than any of the teasing that he received.

The children who had been involved in a game of teasing him about something as insignificant as short pants, had no realization of just how deeply they were hurting him or the magnitude of the burden he carried. The fact that he didn't even have parents seemed a secondary worry to him, but the huge impact of this realization hit the children very hard. I could see the immediate shock and empathy on their faces as I scanned the room.

A silent pact was made that day. These children became fierce in their loyalty to Ben and would not tolerate any more teasing. They became his advocates and included him in all of their sports' groups. He turned out to be a wonderful student with a brilliant sense of humor that began to emerge that term. He was invited to birthday parties and included in playground activities. Over time, Ben wore new pants and the entire situation became history. These children learned a valuable lesson that day.

Listen carefully, forgive yourself and vow to "right the wrong".

It was a wonderful feeling to see Ben graduate three years later and receive the Citizenship Award which he so richly deserved. (It had been a staff and student vote)

Take stock of any habit of thought or action that does not contribute to your happiness, then resolve to change that habit "now". If you fall from grace a few times, do not waste your energy feeling sorry for yourself, and above all, do not get discouraged, but dig right in and continue the practice of replacing the bad habit. Fill your days with constructive thoughts and actions and avoid thinking about that faux-pas again. Gain a new attitude toward life in general! Vow to maintain a positive and happy outlook. Fill yourself with bright new ideas. Accept your peers for who they are and work to lift them up as often as possible. We all love to be encouraged.

Be the encourager!

(3) Be enthusiastic.

This word envelops a true component of success. If we could stay enthusiastic about the goals that we set for ourselves, half of our problem would already be solved. Too often, we start off running, slow down to jogging mode, get tired and begin walking and then just peeter out. It is enthusiasm that keeps us motivated and focused on the task at hand.

Work to keep your students enthused; be enthusiastic yourself!! Remember that modeling is the best way for others to learn from you. Meet your students at the door each morning with a smile on your face and an enthusiastic welcome in your voice. Give them positive body language and they will respond accordingly.

Children will respond much more successfully all day if they are met with a positive manner and an enthusiastic welcome.

If you can exemplify enthusiasm, it will rub off and eventually become a part of your students' nature. Get rid of the negative thoughts. Adopt new phrases that only allow positive thoughts.
"I will study and pass this test" instead of "I'll try and pass this test."
"I am a good listener" instead of "I will try to listen better."

This is an excellent habit to begin and practice all year long. It can make the difference between success and failure throughout a person's life. Enthusiastic people are statistically more healthy, more productive and more successful.

"Genuine enthusiasm isn't something you put on or take off. Genuine enthusiasm is a way of life."

BurkeHedges

(4) Have the Courage to take Action

You will meet many children who practice the bad habit of procrastination. You may even be one of "those" children in a big body. This is one habit that should be dealt with by learning to replace it with action. Teach children to "Do it now" rather than waiting for the last minute. Always plan or outline their assigned tasks. Give them time lines for each part of the project and take the necessary steps to see that the daily planner is used effectively EACH DAY. Chunk projects down into bite-sized pieces that can be "chewed" easily and effectively.

A wise minister reminded his congregation of living in the moment with this expression:

"Yesterday is a canceled check. Today is cash in hand. Tomorrow is a promissory note."

Often students become overwhelmed at the enormity of a project or assignment. Teaching them that small actions over time can create big results is a huge but invaluable lesson that can be used throughout their entire lives. Begin now!

(5) **Teach persistence**

Calvin Coolidge states: "Nothing in the world can take the place of persistence. Talent will not; nothing is more common than unsuccessful people with talent. Genius will not; unrewarded genius is almost a proverb. Education will not; the world is full of educated derelicts. Persistence and determination alone are omnipotent. The slogan 'Press on' has solved and always will solve the problems of the human race."

If children are made aware early, that, with persistence they can accomplish anything, you will find a much more animated, goal-oriented and successful group working in your classroom. I will not take the time to quote some of the many stories of successful people who have accomplished great things through persistence. You probably have a repertoire of stories at hand. Use them whenever you can to inspire your little minions. Take a few minutes per week to read an inspirational story of someone's difficulties and achievements. Inspire and reflect upon the absolute power and results of implementing persistence into your character and your life.

Be persistent!

These 5 habits would be categorized as emotional or character-building. They cannot be seen, only felt and utilized to build the strength of inner self. My list continues with concrete habits that can be evaluated and perused throughout the course of the day or week. Although equally valuable, they rely heavily on the habits already listed.

(6) **Use your daily organizer, planner, whatever you wish to call it.**

When you hand out the daily planner at the beginning of the year, take out your own DayTimer to show the children it's usefulness beyond school and on into adulthood. If you don't have one, GET ONE and start using it. My students get to see the private world of Mrs. Hearn when I flash page after page of events in my life.

-pick up dry cleaning
-dentist appointment 3:15 p.m.
-library meeting 7 p.m.
-write a note to _____ and mail today

By taking a look at all of the activities written in my planner, they can see that I use it daily and it benefits my life because I remember their activities as well.

-hockey game 8:00 Virgil arena

-Spoil-me-day - pick up movie

-visit Leeann's new kitten

I explain the benefits of my planner and my sincere desire for them to achieve the same benefits. When children realize that you are asking them to do the very thing that you do each day, it doesn't become such a burden. It doesn't mean that every child will follow "enthusiastically" in your footsteps, but it will motivate many of them and eventually, for some, it becomes routine.

When introducing the planner, make your expectations very specific.

Instruct children to

-Write down all assignments of the day.

-Keep a log of what's been finished and what needs to be completed. (Checklist)

-Write down any forms that need to be signed and returned

-record the phone numbers of students who may need to be called for a group project.

-any other pertinent school information

Encourage students to add their personal appointments as well.

Example; Call Oma after dinner. Arrange a visit.

I have always insisted that my students get their organizers signed regularly by a parent and often do "spot checks" to insure that parents are actually aware of the work required and being completed. Moms and dads are encouraged not to sign the organizer until all of the homework is accomplished. If it is signed, I am no longer responsible for having to deal with complaints of

"I didn't know that Megan had to complete this work by Monday."

I have had situations where the organizer was signed when the homework was not complete. I then put it right back on the parent's shoulders when acceptable marks were not achieved.

It's an invaluable tool for you to keep parents informed on a daily basis without having to do too much extra work. If you wish to write a note home, it can be added to the organizer where it is easily seen and responded to. The secret is to keep it simple and productive.

51

Often, children are so impressed by your example of using the daily planner that they will follow it because they wish to please you, not because it's for their own good.

Your example and influence often reach far beyond the classroom. I have often had parents ask me to explain something to their child because they felt that I would get a far better response than they would. A few years ago, a frantic mother called me after school. She and her daughter had almost come to blows while deciding on the impending grad dress. She begged me to discuss appropriate graduation dresses with her daughter as she felt that my opinion would be more influential than hers. Apparently "she was an old-fashioned mother who knew nothing about modern day graduations." My student had her heart set on a slinky, strapless gown (Grade 8) and mom was mortified. It turned out that this girl valued my sense of fashion (it seems that I was much cooler and in style) and was very willing to listen to my suggestions. We actually made an evening of shopping together and, with our input, she picked out a beautiful age appropriate gown with spaghetti straps and matching nylon jacket. Mother and daughter had compromised and both were happy with the outcome. Now, I realize that this example is a bit extreme and I am not suggesting that you go shopping with your students but I am suggesting that you do influence them greatly. Keep that in mind!

(7) Find something good that you can do for someone each day and write it down.

This habit is invaluable! It develops character and a love of giving. It is a proven fact of Nature that when you give just for the sake of giving, you will, in time, reap many more benefits than the receiver of your actions. Choose something good that you can do for another and follow up on it.

You can do the same thing for a whole week but for a different person each day.

Example for children: Bake cookies, wrap them individually and give one to someone different each day. (an aunt, grandmother, friend at school, teacher, principal, secretary, custodian)

As a class, we have made lists of "wonderful things to do for wonderful people".

We have participated in "WW Art classes" where we created Wonderful cards for Wonderful people.

One year, my Grade 8 class created a long list of goals and chose yard work as the main focus for their collective "good deed." It was decided that we would organize groups of workers to clean up the huge yard of a local family.

The mother was disabled, therefore physically unable to perform housework and the husband worked full-time and ran the household. (He does an amazing job, by the way!) The students decided that they would rotate housework and yard work for spring "clean up". Each week, a group of six students would meet with rakes in hand and work for approximately two hours. Some of the girls baked cookies at the house or brought already baked treats for the family who always provided pop for the children. Our work was very much appreciated and one evening we found the photographer of our local newspaper in the yard. A group picture was taken and submitted with a lovely tribute to the children. You couldn't have pulled those children off of "Cloud Nine" if you tried. That was such a successful idea that it continued for another family the next year, not because I brought it up but because the Grade 7 students had heard about it and wanted to do the same thing. I was deeply touched and joined my "singing" group of students as they hauled over 45 bags of leaves and branches out of the yard in the following weeks.

It fascinates me how children will volunteer to work so hard to help someone for no other reason than it feels good. The pizza parties provided by the grateful families at the end of the eight weeks were an unexpected immediate reward. The memory of their efforts - forever!

Another wonderful "good deed" was the Grade 8 Christmas tradition. A group of children baked cookies, squares, etc. and brought them to school on a designated evening during the last week before Christmas. We coordinated and wrapped an assortment of these delectable delights on colorful Christmas plates topping them with beautiful bows. The whole group, covered from head to toe in a variety of knitted mufflers, toques, mittens and scarves marched out into the frosty night. A very careful list had been compiled by one of the students who lived in this community. It contained the names of widows/widowers, single people and any others who had recently caused the tiny town's population to jump. Systematically, we visited each designated home, sharing our goodies (being pulled on a sled) and the spirit of the season from our varied selection of Christmas carols. The smiles, tears and grateful hugs of the recipients would long be remembered. A tired, somewhat frozen but elated group of children returned to the school to be driven home by proud, happy parents who saw the joys of community service firsthand. These children had learned and benefited from one of the most valuable lessons we should practice and teach - "be of service to others"

"Whenever there is another human being, there is an opportunity for kindness."

Mother Theresa

SURPRISES - WE LOVE THEM

It is always a wonderful surprise when I receive an unexpected phone call, card, or gift. It picks me up for at least the day but often much longer than that. I know that I am not alone in this. I have often discussed with my students, the human need to feel good and how we can fill that need for someone else for very little effort or cost. Each child comes up with a list of people who may be having a difficult time or someone who could benefit from a surprise. (grandmother, aunt, friend, classmate, etc.) The possibilities are endless. Then we brainstorm fun things to do to "pick them up". Examples: (1) bake cookies and share them (2) create a heartfelt card (I have received many of these from my students over the years and I have kept each one. I read them on "blue" days and they make me feel special) (3) recycle an interesting book (hit used book stores and buy inexpensive copies of your favorite books)

There are so many ways in which we can share a smile. It not only makes the receiver feel good but it does wonders for the giver. It is a proven fact that if you practice this on a regular basis, you will be happier, more organized, and develop a stronger positive attitude in life.

A special student in my last class shared the fruits of his garden with me each day over a one week period. I received a zucchini, a tomato, an eggplant, a squash, and finally a bag of beans. Each day provided a new, unexpected treat and it gave Nicky a chance to share the talents he utilized when he was not in school. He was able to explain the planting process and the correct time to harvest these tasty items. He and his grandmother had spent a lot of time together while gardening and he shared a few of their special stories and new Italian words for my list.

He felt as important in sharing these fruits of his labors with me as I did being the recipient of his hard work and effort. It didn't end there. On many other days throughout the year, I would find a cookie, a cupcake or a little homemade card on my desk from this enthusiastic, amiable young boy. He fully understood and practiced the concept of making someone feel important and both he and I were happier for it. I very much appreciated Nicky's efforts and the wonderful bond he created. He wore a continuous grin because he felt very good about himself and his ability to make others feel good as well. Isn't that what it's all about? Thanks, Nicky!

(8) Learn to listen effectively

Most people would rather talk than listen.
"One does not learn, nor does he enrich his memory, when he is talking."

Howard E. Hill

Listening requires determination and demands a firm, resolute decision to keep one's mouth shut and one's ears open to be fully receptive to intelligent conversation. It demands energy and is actually hard work at first. I would know this firsthand because I still have a problem with "keeping my mouth shut and my ears open" and am continuously working on it.

Paying attention can become a habit if it is taught in the classroom at an early age.

It is a common belief that we are born with a natural ability to listen. I disagree. I have encountered many children who have listened to me but later, don't have a clue what I said. I believe that "Learning to listen 101" should be a part of every teacher's curriculum. I realize that not all children are audio learners and so it becomes much more difficult for those who are not, but it is still possible for them to learn to listen more effectively. How do we do this?

WE CAN IMPROVE LISTENING SKILLS BY...

We can add many different things while we are teaching.For instance:

- **add color to something being discussed**. Print relevant words on brightly colored paper and flash them up once in a while to reinforce and idea or thought; Vanna White style.

- **involve children in the lesson plan.** Have a child or two come up to the front of the class and act out little sections of what is being discussed. Ex. Medieval history - page, knight and their responsibilities. One of my best lessons in discussing the ladder of rank in medieval history was to designate pages, knights and a queen. Pages cleaned boots and stables, were knighted and discussed the attributes and pitfalls of royalty, all in succession. We contributed to, laughed with and enjoyed the various roles that each played. It became a very "fun" lesson and the children were able to remember the various levels of rank during that period of time. A very simple lesson created a memorable moment. Have them often!

- **have children repeat what we have said in their own words**.

Choose a child who has been listening (your intention is not to humiliate, but to instill) and have them interpret what you said. Build a class discussion on this interpretation in order to build a wider scope of understanding.

-have a student draw pictures on the blackboard as you go.

This is a great one for the child who has difficulty paying attention. Give him/her a piece of chalk and allow them to "cartoon it" on the board as you speak. Be sure that they understand that it is a privilege, not a right to do this and silliness is not acceptable. They could lose their chance to come back to the board at a later date.

There are many ways to teach children to listen. Use the ways that suit you best and which are the most effective for the class and age group that you teach. Quite frankly, all of the above methods have been useful right up to Grade 12. If I am teaching an older group of students, I make it more of a "humor thing". They do listen and remember. Years after teaching a particular group of Grade 8 students, I was entertained by a few of them as they recounted the amazing "stick people" lesson that seemed to be firmly implanted in their memory followed by the performance of a song (with actions) created to teach an intricate anatomy lesson in science.

(9) **Learn to study effectively**

This habit should have its beginning during the early years of a child's education and should continue for the lifetime of the learner. **Too many children do not know how to study!**

Many children are able to remember things temporarily and get it on the page for a test but the long-term memory becomes a challenge. How many times have teachers heard about some of their academic students crashing in high school. Often it was due to the fact that they had to actually study and didn't know how. There are too many stories where mothers discuss their children's progress in high school by starting off with "My child was such an amazing student in elementary school, but now that he is in high school, the teachers don't seem to care enough about him and he is not experiencing success at all."

Having never taught their child, I listen patiently and with the understanding that they are indeed concerned, but **it is seldom the fault of the high school teachers and I tell them so**. We must all work to support each other in the field of education and assist parents in realizing some of their own fundamental responsibilities.

It is our responsibility to support all teachers, both elementary and secondary

Often, those in the secondary panel teach their subject area to hundreds of children on rotary. They are just as concerned about the progress and success of each individual but they cannot spare the time to teach the study skills that should already be in place. The luxury of getting to know each student as individually as the elementary teachers did is not viable due to time constraints. They are just as concerned about the progress and success of each individual but they must handle things differently. There is, and rightfully so, more responsibility placed on the child as they grow older. It is a natural progression. A very important component of secondary school is to learn independence, something that I, as a mother who wishes to help her children succeed, have had to wrestle with from time to time myself. If you are a parent, look at the foundational skills of your own children and work to improve their study habits as well as those of your students. Prepare them for secondary and post-secondary schooling by teaching and reviewing a solid formula for successful studying. The following one is the best that I have found. It is not complicated and can begin in the early years of schooling.

Formula for successful studying.

(1)   Read the book, lesson or assignment carefully.

(2)   Question everything that you have read - go back paragraph by paragraph and question all of its points.

(3)   Restate the material in your own words. This is where my point form notes come in as I teach children to rewrite the information in point form IN THEIR OWN WORDS. A goal is for your students to become familiar with the dictionary and thesaurus as early as possible. They provide invaluable information for point form rewriting.

(4)   Review what you have read. Read it to yourself or to a partner. Have them question you about the information but REVIEW the way that will help you to remember it best.

If you can follow this process with experience, the lesson is learned.

Dramatic presentations, experiments, field trips and movies or film clips are wonderful ways in which to experience and review lessons. Any time you can add visuals to a lesson, it becomes part of a bigger learning process.

Teach children not to cram for tests but to review on a daily basis. Whenever they have a few spare minutes in the day, remind them to review that geography or history lesson. Make it a regular habit and it will become a good one that can be used throughout all of their years of learning.

If you can afford a ten minute "study period" each day or a few times a week, you can actually go through these steps with them and teach them the concept of regular review reading. Make it a part of your "good habits" lessons and it will prove a beneficial strategy throughout life. While they are reading, have them write very brief point form notes on a separate paper. This page can become a short summary of each section studied. They then use these short, faster "study notes" for upcoming tests.

I can't stress this formula for studying enough!!!!

If children can learn these simple steps, THEIR ABILITY TO STUDY AND MEMORIZE INFORMATION WILL GREATLY IMPROVE. You will have performed a great service in their lives and the teachers of their future will be grateful. The trick is to also get parents on board. If they can realize the importance of this formula and how it will benefit their children in the future, they may begin practicing it with them at home. It doesn't take much time and they will see positive results. You can even invite interested parents to a small "study habits workshop" one evening. You can't even imagine the points that you'll score with these people as you go through a few sample exercises with them and instruct them on how easy it is to help their child. Never be afraid to show small acts of kindness and to give of yourself and your own time. Most parents will appreciate it more than you can imagine. I know that, as a parent, I do!

There are various **HOOKS** we can use to memorize information.

(1) **Visual Memory Hooks**

KTAVOG are the first letters in the **Learning Styles of children** (Chapter 13)

Visual hooks are an excellent way to teach the visual learner. The majority of children are visual learners. Have your students create some of their own for an art and _____ lesson.

(2) **Mnemonics**: Memory Hooks
A mnemonic is a technique or system of improving memory by the use of certain formulas.
Examples are:
Cell Division
Mitosis: "**I**mmodest **P**aul **M**ade **A**nother **T**ouchdown" for Interphase Prophase, Metaphase, Anaphase, and Telophase

Music Notes -notes listed on the lines of the staff (from the bottom up)
Every **G**ood **B**oy **D**eserves **F**udge

General Tree Categories
"Deciduous Trees drop their leaves. Conifers bear cones."

Geography
"HOMES" is an acronym for the names of the Great Lakes
Huron, Ontario, Michigan, Erie, Superior
Asia is the shortest name for the largest continent

Grammar
"**D**elicious **MINTS**" is a way to recall the use of capitalization:
D is days of the week;
M is months of the year;
I is used when it is a word;
N is names of people, places, things, or ideas;
T is titles of books, plays;
S is the start of a sentence.

Spelling
There are so many different spelling phrases that can be used that I challenge you to fill in many more blanks here.
i before e except after c

_____

_____

Use Every Trick in the Book and then some

As a teacher, surrounded by other professionals, you will find many tricks of the trade; memory hooks can be used in every subject area. Music jingles and catchy phrases have been concocted for almost everything there is and if you haven't found one, make one up or use it as a project for your students.

These are the things that make learning fun and help children realize that they have a wonderful memory mechanism within themselves. They just have to tap into their wealth of knowledge and with your help, everyone can do it! Implant this idea into the consciousness of your students. Teach them to believe in themselves and their abilities.

THE CONSCIOUS MIND

"If you think you are beaten, you are;
If you think you dare not, you don't;
If you'd like to win but you think you can't,
It's almost a cinch you won't;
If you think you'll lose, you've lost,
For out in the world, you'll find
Success begins with a fellow's will;
It's all in the state of mind."

Selected - by Venice Bloodworth

"Habit"

"The appreciation of the good and beautiful is intensified when we are confronted with our daily problems. It may sound trite to say practice thinking in the high vibratory altitude when situations appear to be unbearable - it's so easy to let oneself drift into the low depression areas.

Just as the feeling of clean teeth and sweet smelling mouth becomes a habit with daily brushing, so can you brush the decay out of your thinking before the wrong thoughts get a chance to make a painful cavity."

Joanne D'Alton Clancy
"a way out from in"

CHAPTER SEVEN

Building Confidence in the Classroom

Do not confuse this section of the book with Building Self-Esteem as I will spend a good many pages discussing that topic later on. Confidence does not necessarily mean self-esteem.

Confidence: assurance, presumption; self-reliance, hence courage or boldness
Self-Esteem: a good opinion of oneself; an overestimate of oneself

In this section of the book, I wish to stress the building of "self-reliance, courage, boldness" in a positive way. The following pages introduce various "tried and true" strategies to help build that confidence.

Self-esteem becomes an even bigger issue as we can often see "bullies" exuding large amounts of negative boldness and courage on the playground. It seems that they are filled with confidence when, in fact, a proven theory states that **"bullies are often so unsure of themselves that they must make other children feel bad in order to give themselves a feeling of power and importance"**. Children with positive self-esteem are supportive and work to build others up.

Building positive confidence in children at any age level should be a goal for every teacher.

There are many simple classroom lessons and techniques to help children build confidence.

(1) Blab a blurb

This is just a quirky expression that I use. Make up your own "fun" expression. This allows children to relate something special to their peers. It could be something that they did on the weekend, perhaps participate in a sporting event that was exciting or went very well.

In my last placement, I taught many boys who played hockey and it was interesting to hear their reports of the games, especially when I had been a spectator. Some students participate in amazing activities after school and it gives you a more diverse insight.(soccer, gymnastics, band, lacrosse) Often, you are totally unaware of their talents. In the junior grades, this "blurb" time becomes a very exciting thing. Often, children will bring pictures or other memorabilia from the place they visited. I listened to a very "shy" child recount her version of Shaw Festival's "Peter Pan". Her animated, detailed summary was so interesting that it inspired me to purchase tickets for my mom and I to see it. I limit the "blurbs" to five minutes and I choose a few students each week. Keep a record of which students have presented in order to include all students and not zone in on the same ones. You will always have "regulars" whose hands will shoot up daily. They must be taught to prioritize their events and report less often, allowing others to have a chance. Giving them a day's notice allows you to control the number of students and the time they will present. I have incorporated it into my timetable at times throughout the school year.

If no one presents, I use this time for "study and review". It insures that I will make the time for these things. If I don't schedule it in, I often forget to "do it".

(2) **Student of the Week**

Each week, I choose one student who has accomplished something worthy of attaining the title "Student of the Week". It can be **any** positive thing. The goal here is to have each and every student become the recipient of this title. A "special" bulletin board is dedicated for this honor. The winner is announced on Friday and given the weekend to search for five pictures to display for the next week. On Friday, when the new winner is announced, the present "student of the week" stands at the board, describes the events, people and/or pets found in each picture and answers any questions that their peers may have for them. All but one of the photos are removed, making room for the next grouping. By keeping one photo on the board, the "Board of winners" becomes a continuous positive reinforcement.

The "mini speech" topic is clear, they know the information well and there is very little room for embarrassment or faltering. This provides an opportunity for children to present information confidently, knowing that they are able to answer the questions geared around their lives.

Accompanying the announcement is a reward of some kind. Mine is usually a chocolate bar but I've heard that some teachers actually frown on rewarding children with chocolate (yeesh!) so you can use your own judgement. My students have never turned down a candy bar or Tootsie pop. I keep a variety in my desk at all times. I may mention that a few more times in the book. Candy has always worked for me, although I have been known to use other types of rewards. (pizza lunches, bags of chips, movie passes, a free pop, special duties and responsibilities during school, etc.)

(3) **Peer reading buddies**

The fact that many children are not reading as much as they should is a serious concern of mine and I encourage my students to do it all costs. I hunt for books, appropriate magazines, comic books and any other reading material that would prompt my "difficult readers" to join in the reading program. I comb flea markets, garage sales and used book stores. I seldom pay full price for a book and I have a network of parents, former and present, who do the same for me. I visit a unique "gently used" book store on a regular basis and put in requests. "Hannelore Headley's" is a wonderful example of the many resources available to us in our communities.

Our class library has always been a separate entity from the school library and I encourage children to use every library available to them. I proofread unknown books in order to screen their appropriateness for school because I am an avid believer in the notion that what children read often impacts future interests and actions. Reading more wholesome books at a younger age develops proper vocabulary and values during the formative years. It allows for better decision-making as they grow old enough to make their own choices for books and movies. Students should be made aware of appropriate standards and choose books accordingly.

I have been pleasantly shocked from time to time when a student, who experiences difficulty achieving success in school, chooses to read such books as "The Hobbit" or "Lord of the Rings" and enjoys them immensely. (Quite frankly, I had difficulty understanding the world of those little creatures myself). Aren't books wonderful?

> ***"The person who can read and doesn't is just as bad off as the person who can't read."***
>
> **Anonymous**

Silent reading during class is very important and often gives you important insights to a child's interest. You can individualize projects and presentations much more easily when you know some of the preferred reading materials that certain students zone in on. Often, this will be the only time that some students read to themselves. It is surprising how many parents confess that their children do not read at home. They can't seem to pull them away from the television or computer screen. Taking a book, sitting in a quiet place, and reading for even a few minutes each day is invaluable to a child's learning. Herein lies future vocabulary, sentence structure and a world of fantasy and fiction. These are vital components of a child's progress in the world of building language and knowledge. Make sure that you do not "fudge" on the time allotted for silent reading and, above all, **allot silent reading time!**

Reading aloud is promoted and, knowing that this is where a lot of reading breaks down, students are "buddied" up. I have them practice reading to each other for prepared reading work, especially drama. Partners are changed more frequently at the beginning of the year in order to match the best combination of students to work well together.

They crawl into corners of the classroom, the library or the hallway (careful not to disturb other classes). They confide in each other and feel free to express their fears of reading.

In time, you start to see the partners who "click". Confidence grows and children take greater risks. Ultimately, a trust factor develops, allowing for mistakes and faltering in a non-threatening setting. Students help each other overcome fears. Inflection is added and oral presentations for the class are prepared. Noise levels go up but learning gears up even more.

I no longer support the idea that children should be chosen at random to read unprepared pieces of literature in front of the class.

Children should always be given the opportunity to prepare oral work ahead of time. The piece becomes more interesting to listen to, generally contains inflection and creative reading is the result, as opposed to a stressful, inaccurate effort complete with stumbling and frustration, ending in humiliation. There is nothing worse than sitting in a class listening to a poor reader struggling to plow through an assigned passage. That is the best way to turn a child off of reading. It is a cruel punishment and I believe it to be criminal.

CHILDREN SHOULD NEVER BE PUT ON THE SPOT TO READ UNPREPARED WORK OUT LOUD IN FRONT OF THEIR CLASSMATES

Over the years, there have been many discoveries of great speaking talent in children who presented shy, hesitant behaviors when asked to orally answer a question. These same children, when allowed to **prepare** an opinion or reading passage produced such profound, confident results that I learned never again to "put them on the spot".

It was a learning experience for me and I apologize profusely to any students who were asked to read at random during my early years of teaching and who remember it as a dreadful ordeal.

It was a mistake; something that I truly regret but I have learned and I hope to pass my knowledge on to those teachers who have not yet discovered the truth of this lesson.

Public speaking should definitely be encouraged and you will have a much more receptive audience when you build confidence in each and every one of your speakers.

(4) **Primary Book Presentations**

I have used this exercise with intermediate and senior students but I suppose that it would work just as well with juniors.

The entire class heads down to the library and each student looks for an interesting **primary** book. It should be easy for them to read. It should have colorful, interesting illustrations and it should not be so lengthy that it becomes boring to the primary listener.

Students begin to make choices and read them to their "buddy". After a few selections, they choose the one that is the most interesting and enjoyable. Each child should have a book when leaving the library. (I have, on occasion, allowed a few students to bring in a book from home.) Perhaps it's repetition made it more comfortable a read than those found in the library or perhaps it was just a favorite that they had grown up with and wanted to share with others.

The following assignment is three-fold.

A) The book chosen is designated for a Grade 1,2 or 3 class. Students are directed to create two worksheets coinciding with their choice of book. These sheets must teach a valuable lesson for the Grade level they will be instructing. The pages must be neat, clearly printed (often on the computer) and easily understood. A class rubric is created!

Worksheets should contain questions, number exercises, a coloring assignment, matching characters with events or other pertinent primary lesson material. When completed, they are handed in, evaluated and returned. Any necessary corrections are made and sufficient copies are photocopied for the chosen class.

B) Students must be able to read the book aloud with proper inflection to create an interesting presentation for the class. We practice this in our own classroom first. Each person sits at the front of the class and presents their book and lessons to their peers. Students then evaluate the presentation, providing **constructive** criticism. This becomes a valuable experience, teaching all members of the class the importance of input from others and how to accept it graciously, not defensively. Corrections are made accordingly. The worksheets are handed out and explained in detail and students then question their relevance to the curriculum and the effectiveness of subsequent evaluation.

C) Each student is then responsible for approaching a primary teacher and scheduling an appointment to present their book to the class. A huge timetable is set up as a calendar and put up on the bulletin board for reference. Primary teachers have always welcomed this opportunity for student input and are generally very open to this assignment. The student presents the book to the class at the allotted time, assigns the two worksheets and supervises the children as they complete the work. Worksheets are collected and the student takes them home to carefully evaluate them according to the criteria set out in the plan. Students are encouraged to attach positive stickers or stamps on the pages as a way of rewarding the children's efforts. A set of marks, along with the evaluated papers, is then returned to the primary teacher.

My students are evaluated according to their previously prepared rubric. This exercise provides an enjoyable learning experience for each student and I've not yet evaluated an unsuccessful presentation. Talk about building confidence. These students become teachers for a period or two and they love the responsibility.

(5) Debates! Debates! Debates!

One of the more successful lessons that I have found is giving children topics that they can become passionate about and then having them debate the issues. For example; when discussing human rights (Amnesty International is delighted to hear from teachers and provides a wealth of information to the school), children are given a list of priorities in life.

-the right to be protected
-the right to proper nutrition
-the right to be educated
-the right to exercise freedom of speech
-the right to be housed
-the right to exercise freedom of religion and so on...

Human rights is a very important topic that children in this country should be made aware of. There are excellent web sites that provide vital information on many world issues including child labor laws and women's rights. It always amazes me to find the interest that lies within the class as we delve into some of these virtually unknown areas. A colorful and diverse unit can be created for history, English, geography and even guidance.

Again, have fun mixing and matching as you discuss important and interesting issues happening right now. Bring newspapers to school and find articles on a daily basis. (A newspaper unit is also extremely interesting and fun.)

Each child chooses the one "right" that they feel is the most important to them. A good habit to get into is to write the list of topics on the board followed by a brief brainstorming session in order for students to get their "jump start" on building ideas. Allow for personal knowledge and information to be discussed as children become more comfortable with the topics at hand. They then filter into the community to build support for their "right", compiling notes and creating valid arguments for their choice. It becomes interesting to watch them promote their ideas to each other, swaying back and forth in search of the validity required for sincere belief. It is this sincere belief that allows them to debate. A noisy environment should be tolerated for this portion of the assignment as students accumulate more information and answers to their questions. Papers are then written during a more formal, quiet time and students "prepare their argument."

Let the debates begin! This can be accomplished any way you see fit. Formal debates are a useful tool for intermediate classes as they prepare them for future debating teams. Debate outlines are available at your Board offices or even on line. (Look under UN Debate on the Internet) A much less complicated format can be used for junior and even primary students.

When the debating process is over, students condense their conclusions into persuasive paragraphs. These can be read at assemblies, during the morning announcements, or to other classes. One year, our principal created a ballot and introduced the topics for a school vote in order to prioritize their importance. The senior students, having debated the list of the "rights of a child", read their presentations at an assembly. Children listened, chose the right they favored, and voted. The votes were tallied and the priorities were listed in order of greatest to least. It gave serious "food for thought" to the entire student body in a powerful way. It was a meaningful, informative way for the students to connect with world issues.

Debate results also create information for teaching graphs, surveys, sharing with reading buddies, and the list goes on. Students soon forget their fear of speaking as they dig in to convince others that the "side" they favor is the correct one.

Depending upon the age of the children, you may use a multitude of wonderful issues to debate in a more open forum.

My intermediates love to debate

(1) should schools have uniforms?

(2) should there be security checks upon entering all schools?

(3) what criteria mandates expulsion from school?

(4) is suspension from school the right answer?

In secondary classes, much heavier issues like abortion or premarital sex can be challenging but tread carefully and be sure that your students are mature enough to build arguments based upon "supportive information and statistics" rather than just opinion.

A fundamental lesson here is to teach your students to learn that, when they are debating, they must compile accurate facts, statistics and general knowledge to support both sides of the argument.

I have often asked students to fully research a topic. I then choose the side they will debate. It can never be too personal as they must be able to support the assigned view with correct data and examples. A trip to the public library becomes a most valuable resource lesson. Microfiche and newspaper articles from the past years contain much of the controversial opinions and facts that can be used for more serious debates. UN Debate teams are a national student forum and provide educational opportunities for growth around the country.

Libraries will book research time and provide a specialist to teach students how to use the various resources in the building. It is surprising how many children have never been to a public library, let alone know how to utilize it in their studies. Debates are a fun and interesting way to build confidence and curriculum. Enjoy it and remember, **you can never make a mistake because it's debatable!**

(6) Dramatic presentations

Often, a child who feels uncomfortable speaking in front of his peers, will feel much less so being part of a dramatic presentation. It is your task to mix groups carefully, allowing some of the stronger role models to provide direction, encouragement and much needed support. There will be some occasions where you can take particular students aside (you will come to know and trust certain children) asking them for special "assistance" in building confidence and self-esteem in another student. Generally, they are thrilled to be asked and eager to be part of an "undercover" support system. The willingness of children to help others never ceases to amaze me. They volunteer for so many things that I am often brought to tears by their eagerness. Wouldn't it be wonderful if this desire to help could be supported and carried on in such an innocent, unconditional way throughout their lives? With the help and support of peers, many children overcome their fears in tackling a dramatic role. What a thrill it is for a teacher to watch a reticent child perform an oral presentation without fear or hesitation. This builds confidence!

(7) **Theater sports**

Incorporate theater sports into your drama class. Assign children "an appropriate" topic and create the scene for them. Make it fairly structured because if you don't set certain boundaries and limitations for them, things are apt to get pretty wild. **It has become an obvious fact during the Spoken Word Festivals that certain boundaries should be set for theater sports.**

Unfortunately, children are becoming more and more exposed to television shows that go beyond the normal boundaries set for children's viewing. I don't wish to name them, but I believe that we, as educators, understand what is and what is not appropriate for children. We screen our movies and television excerpts very carefully in schools and I believe that parents should do the same, but I digress.

Change roles within the group. Allow students some preparation time at the beginning of this program but eventually take it away, allowing for more and more ad-libbing. Students who exhibit shyness at the beginning will have an opportunity to grow into these exercises and actually become more confident "as time goes by" (now, there is a wonderful TV program. Dame Dench is magnificent.)

(8) **Spirit assemblies**

As I have mentioned and will continue to do so, my last principal of five years was a very energetic, positive leader. She believed in school spirit and we had spirit days and spirit assemblies on a regular basis. These assembly times are set aside for students to share their talents and accomplishments. Teachers are asked to add their student contributions to "the list".

Assemblies are capped at a designated time allotment and quickly filled. These group assemblies become the perfect arena for that "shy" student to exhibit what she has accomplished.

(I put the word "shy" in brackets because I don't believe that children are born "shy". I believe that it is a characteristic that they are "given" at an early age and, through reinforcement 'my child is very shy', they tend to develop the components of being "shy".)

Never tell a youngster that he/she is shy as they will come to believe that label and actually present all of its characteristics in their personality. I deal with that later on in Chapter 22, "Building Self Esteem".

These less gregarious children often hide their talents but here, we can scout them out. They are given the opportunity to share whatever it is they have written, created or accomplished with the student body. (often, it is a poem, a short story, a painting or an honored medal won at a sporting event. Even better if it is an unknown talent, perhaps discovered after school by a sleuth student.) Make it a game to see who can find hidden talents in the classroom. Because it is a common occurrence to have students share, it becomes less of a burden to this "quiet" group of children and they feel more at ease. If we follow the cliché, **practice makes perfect**, we know that, through positive experiences, the confidence of children will automatically build.

Our school has had wonderful spirit assemblies and I have many fond memories of children shouting their practiced mottos and cheers for their teams or "houses". Every child, Grades 1-8, is part of a "house". During special spirit assemblies, "houses" and their leaders (a designated teacher or two) often sit together. Throughout the year, these groups compete in sporting events, winter carnivals and other school activities. Various spectacular paraphernalia is worn to represent "the house". Children of all ages band together to compete and have oodles of fun.

Senior students become acquainted with the primary and junior children and nice bonds are created. It seems that the playground is a safer place to be as the older ones look out for their younger counterparts. Many positive factors result from Spirit Assemblies. We had a lot of fun at this school and it verifies a truism: a staff that works and plays together, creates a more safe and happy environment for children.

(9) **Spirit days**

I have been known to arrive at school sporting huge multi-colored curlers in my hair, fluffy floppy-eared bunny slippers on my feet, and a turquoise, chenille bathrobe wrapped over colorful Mickey Mouse waffle pajamas. It's Pajama Day and everyone in the **whole** school is having fun...or are they?

Do you plan to be the teacher who enters the school and frowns ever so slightly at the antics of those courageous souls who will cause laughter and glee throughout the day? DON'T BE!!!!!!

Teachers need to get with it and prove to the "kids" that they are willing to make fools of themselves at the expense of fun and spirit. It is harmless and makes such a huge impact on your students that they will never forget you. Do you honestly think that children will remember all of your extraordinary math and science lessons? Not unless they were as fun and ridiculous as your Pajama Day get-up!

Children need to see our humorous side. They need to know that we the teachers, can have fun, and they will pack that morsel of information into their memory bank far more effectively than any academic lesson we ever taught them. I know that I'll never forget the sight of two male teachers, dressed in long black wigs and matching leather riding tricycles on to a stage while the staff band (made up of a drummer, three guitarists and two go-go dancers) played, sang and gyrated to "Born to Be Wild" by Steppenwolf. The crowd went wild and the teachers wore smiles for weeks. We were a hit and the kids loved it! Don't be afraid to take reasonable risks because they are the way to develop stronger bonds with your students. They will love your enthusiasm. I refer to this wonderful emotion "enthusiasm" often because it is a word that should become a part of your consciousness, character and life.

**"Genuine enthusiasm isn't something you put on or take off...
Genuine enthusiasm is a way of life."**

Burke Hedges

*The fastest way to build self-confidence
is to be willing to take a risk
without knowing how something will turn out,
yet knowing that you will
learn from the process!*

Don Wolfe

A few moments ago, you read about teachers' antics on Spirit Days. Teachers should not be afraid to take reasonable risks. If you have always been afraid to "get silly" or "let your hair down" in front of others, now is the time for change. You must be the leader and be willing to take reasonable risks because it is an extremely important concept for children to learn.

WE should not be afraid to take REASONABLE RISKS.

"A reasonable risk is one where you know that you can accept the worst while choosing to go for the best." D. Wolfe

In order to reinforce this, have your students prepare the answers to the following questions and then, one by one, stand in front of the class to answer them.

(1) What do I love to do?

This is an easy question requiring little effort or knowledge. It does not put stress on any child and they should be comfortable in sharing that information with their peers.

(2) What am I good at?

A little bragging never hurt anyone. This is a nice opportunity for all of you to hear a few things that may surprise you. This question could require some encouragement on your part and always be there to physically support the child with a question or a positive comment.

(3) What do I want to learn to be good at?

Your student has to put some thought and effort into answering this question. They have now created a goal, one which you could use in your goal-setting journal (I will get to that later on in the book). An important point to note here is that each student will have a desire to be better at something. It puts all children on an equal playing field. Even the most popular, "perfect" person in the class will reveal a desire to improve something and that makes the more insecure student see an approachable person standing in front of them. I use this example because I have taught children who did not feel worthy to be part of a popular group. They felt insecure and often ugly or "no good." By being put in the same position as those in "the in-crowd", they began to realize that everyone has needs, desires and flaws. Some children can actually find their way out of this negative, insecure state by going through many of the exercises and activities outlined in this and the "Building Self-Esteem" chapters. Remember, it is your job to maintain a positive outlook and an enthusiastic approach to all of the learning that is going on. (Is it easy? No, but it is very rewarding when changes take place.)

> *"You can get better...or you can get bitter."*
>
> Anonymous

(4) **What don't I like about myself?**

Here is "the kicker". This is the toughest question that your students will have to tackle and again, you will be surprised at some of the answers you hear. It's time to get down and dirty and often children are very hard on themselves. They will begin to reveal an honesty that can surprise even their peers. Some will not be able to deal with this in front of the class and that is understandable. They may say, "There isn't anything I don't like about myself." Chalk that up to the fear of vulnerability and allow them to have a seat. Don't make them feel badly about not wishing to participate.

The class clown will often make jokes when it comes to this type of honesty because he is not ready or often able to deal with reality. The more courageous children will open the gates and eventually, all children will recognize qualities that they would like to change.

Some may never say them out loud, but I guarantee, they will think about it and once it begins in their thought process, it will be mulled over and over. You may even see a change in that student who could not voice his desire to change something negative. The most popular students are generally quite vocal and will offer honest information about themselves because they already have confidence and very little fear. Again, this sets a wonderful example of how **we all need to improve** and your class will benefit from this activity.

CAN YOU SEE WHAT I SEE?

From the previous exercise, you will have an idea of how your students perceive themselves. In Jack Canfield's Binder on Building Self-Esteem, you will find a vast number of sheets which can be used to glean this information. Get to know the likes and dislikes of your students, find out what bothers them and what insecurities they are dealing with. Be sure to look for their strengths and weaknesses.

Create situations in the classroom and the school where your children can shine. Find things in them that they cannot see and build them up in those areas. Example: Nicky's gardening skills.

If you wish to use visualization techniques on a mild level, have the class visualize a goal that they have set for themselves. Begin with an easy visualization (seeing a lemon, touching it, cutting it open and watching it drip, licking the juice etc.) Have all of the children on board and watch their faces to see how many of them are actually able to "see" what you are talking about and build it gradually until it can become a goal-setting experience. There are many good books on visualization but check with your school principal before delving into that area as some school districts carry limitations on this type of teaching.

I have been fortunate enough to have used visualization fairly successfully when it came to track and field, hockey tournaments and music concerts. Students were able to "see" themselves performing well and doing their best. They envisioned the results of being the best that they could be and felt the applause and admiration of their audiences. It can be a very powerful tool in all divisions of both elementary and secondary school.

I cannot stress this enough

Find and build positives in your students on a regular basis. There are some children who don't even realize that they have any. They are your challenges!! They will make you grow!

"We all live under the same sky...but we do not all have the same horizon."

Konrad Adenauer

77

CHAPTER EIGHT
Don't Re-Invent the Wheel

Now, ask yourself. How old is this profession?
How many teachers have traveled through this profession?
How many educators are presently in this profession?
How many lesson plans do you think are out there?

Let's look at resources.

1) textbooks with matching teacher resource books, tapes, CDs
2) curriculum compatible documents and units compiled by independent, knowledgeable educators and private businesses
3) unit plans (found on the web sites of all Boards in Ontario)
4) theme sheets and coloring books (can even be found in books at K-Mart)
5) exercises and games (written by the hundreds and kept in school libraries)
6) workbooks filled with worksheets to be photocopied at will
7) photocopiable material (this is becoming more and more available as many authors invite you to share their materials, knowing that the importance of it is to get it out there - just check carefully to make sure that it is photocopy approved)
8) actual curriculum documents being provided by the Board which can be used on a daily basis. All of the lessons are clearly marked, overheads are included, pre-tests, post-tests and evaluation sheets all come as part of the package. I suggest that you add your personal touches to these but they are there for you. Less stress!

You should be getting the general idea by now. There are hundreds and hundreds of completed lesson plans everywhere around you. **Don't get stressed out because you think there are not going to be enough materials for you to teach "that subject".**

Whenever you are preparing a unit for your class, log on to your Board's web site and look for ones that are already prepared and neatly compiled for you. **Download all available materials**. You don't have to follow them lesson by lesson but you can certainly mix and match and, in a pinch, use them verbatim. (If you notice, I like that "verbatim" word and that whole mix and match thing works well with all sorts of mediums).

I have worked with many teachers who have been flattered when I expressed a desire to borrow and implement their units. I, in turn, was only too happy to share my many hours of research with someone who would share with their class as well. Many children benefited from my many hours of preparation even after I had finished teaching that subject area.

Take "archeology" for instance. I have never had a serious interest in archeology but I've heard the children express an interest in it. I knew that my unit would contain the facts, a few interesting exercises, and perhaps culminated in a project that the children would have researched. It seemed as though it could become an interesting unit but I wasn't sure how to "get into it" and where to get started. My goal was to make it memorable, not just factual.

There are many of These Teachers

I remembered that, early in my career, I had met a teacher who had actually gone on a dig in Egypt and had put together a wide variety of materials and lesson plans. We had met at a conference and her stories were fascinating. I called her and found that the unit she had prepared suited both the junior and intermediate levels. Upon adapting it into my program, it became one of the favorite units in a particular special ed. class that I taught. She summarized the unit by coming in as a guest speaker to answer all of the questions that this curious class had to offer. It was gratifying to see that much enthusiasm and excitement in the group.

She had been thrilled that I could use it and I received her permission to pass it on. Her generosity has allowed her talents in that area to be passed on and taught to a multitude of eager, excited children.

Many good principals are often very supportive in allowing their teachers to visit other classrooms or even other schools in order to share. It strengthens the programs being taught and it builds a very interesting curriculum. Inner school coverage can usually be provided

Principals love to hear parents discuss the wonderful learning that their children are experiencing in a class. It builds the positive base that every school needs and teachers can always use a pat on the back.

I have even had a principal come in to cover my class in order for me to observe a "math whiz" teacher at another school. (Anything to help the cause for my Grade 8 class) She enjoyed spending time with my students and I picked up some very valuable math tips and worksheets.

On the other hand, I have met a few tenacious teachers who were unwilling to share their units with anyone and I chalk that up to their ignorance in not realizing how valuable shared resources can be. I just shrug my shoulders and hope that one day they will see the true benefits of sharing ideas and plans with their peers. Some of us are still in the infant stages of learning but we are all learning. I wonder how stressful planning must be for them because they are obviously writing all of their own units and wouldn't dare "borrow", would they?

The most important point here is to **avoid stress**. If life can be made easier because someone else put together a wonderful unit for your use, what could you possibly have to gain by trying to re-create it during a stressful time in your year?

If you have the time and the inclination to create a masterful unit, **DO IT**, otherwise piggy back yourself into a comfortable situation for the time being. Give other teachers the credit they deserve!!! If someone has created this poignant unit and has shown the courtesy of putting it out there for you; support them, honor their contribution and use it.

It is very important for us to learn that we are among a large organization of valuable teachers and all of our efforts should be celebrated, not ignored because "we want to do it ourselves." There will be plenty of opportunities to create your own personal lesson plans and units, to build a library of associated pictures, graphs, documents, resources, review sheets, and tests. The ultimate goal is to share meaningful, enjoyable learning experiences with your students and if it means borrowing materials among yourselves; ENJOY!!!!!

CHAPTER NINE

PLANNING

"If you fail to plan, you are planning to fail." Jack Canfield

I hope that you are a noted planner.

"Ask Alice to have Christmas dinner this year. I know it's July but she's a planner."

If this is something that people kid you about, make fun of, or even acknowledge about you,

"it's a good thing".

Many of the finest, most organized teachers that I have ever worked with are people who have been diagnosed with ADHD. In order to achieve success in life, "ADHD people" must learn to accommodate their wealth of energy and creativity. It must be harnessed, organized and channeled into a constructive way of life. As I am one of these people, I speak from experience when I say that lists, daily planners, calendars and a need to be organized are a way of life.

Have I been teased or been made fun of? Most certainly! Do I get the job done? Always!

Do I always say "yes" and accept the offer of an added responsibility? NO!

Therein lies the secret. Accept only what you feel capable of handling and accomplishing well!

LEARN TO SAY NO but, in the same vein, learn to say yes to the things you can handle. When you have accepted the task, however, be the most organized person you can be and complete it successfully. **It is one of the keys to being a great teacher**. If you are not an organized person, start setting mini-goals for yourself to build the skills necessary to become organized. Start using a daily planner, set up calendars for special events and dates and make sure that you can always see the color of your desk. Follow these simple steps to achieve organization in your planning.

Make a plan for the week

-include short term goals
-complete your daybook (I discuss the daybook in this chapter)
-organize all of the events, assemblies, sports activities, choirs, or other for that week

Continue with your **monthly plan**

-create an overview of your theme for the subjects you teach
-any upcoming special events, trips
-create your monthly newsletter and type it up
-transfer your planned time lines and deadlines into your daybook

Understand that when you transfer these dates into your daybook, they must be flexible **and merely represent a plan** because school activities can often thwart a good plan. You will have assemblies, fire drills, unexpected guest speakers, illness ... to try to "mess up your plan" so you must be flexible. It can change like the weather so "be prepared". Those girl guides and boy scouts are really onto something.

> *"If you don't know where you're going, you're never gonna get there."*
>
> Yogi Berra

Create a long-term or yearly plan which can be used as a reference to keep you on track. It should clearly outline (not be terribly detailed) all of your intentions for the year and should include the major skills as outlined in the curriculum document for the individual subject areas. They are officially known as long range plans and should be available for interested parents who wish to "organize their child's studying" throughout the year.

LONG RANGE PLANS ARE A MUST

Example: Let's look at an example of long range plans for a Grade 4 class for music

September-October	November-December	January-February
-Time signatures -two-part harmony -begin note keeping	-oral choir preparation -learning to recognize musical notation in a piece of music -memorize notes on the staff	-study of instruments -create instruments -point form notes -project due Feb.20

March-April	May-June
-spring concert -partner songs -presentation Apr.25	-study musical "Little Mermaid" -learn three songs from musical -project - plot graph and character study of Little Mermaid -point form notes reviewed -students work in groups - learning skills evaluated -oral presentations

I have not included all of the details of the skills required for the Grade 4 music program as they will be listed in individual lesson plans and in the curriculum itself. When planning and writing out my short and long range plans, I check off the skills in the curriculum guide as I incorporate them into my lessons. You can even photocopy the page directly out of the guide and make it the first page of your binder, highlighting each skill as you teach it. (This is an excellent way to keep track of everything and have it handy.) The next year, you begin with a new page and so on...

My junior music binder becomes the resource binder for the entire junior music curriculum. It contains handouts, information and resource materials as well as individual lesson plans that clearly define particular skills (I often leave a folder containing a few general handouts and worksheets for any supply teacher who may have to cover my class during a trip or an unforeseen absence).

My binder is divided into different sections ranging from notation and theory , information on instruments, and materials for the periods of music being taught in the junior grades. (medieval, renaissance and baroque)

There are written notes with missing blanks for students to fill in and there are pop quiz sheets to review the lessons that have been taught.

The following list will help you to collect and build your resources in the subject area of your choice. (I have used music here but it's pretty straightforward for any subject)

(1)   Collect "game pages" which provide an entertaining, yet informative reviews of lessons. These are often available at workshops and professional development meetings.

(2)   Whenever I find an interesting sheet in someone's folder or portfolio, I ask to reproduce it and add it to my binder.

(3)   Whenever a new student arrives, I ask for their notebook to see if I can use any of the sheets that they may have in it.

(4)   I contact other music teachers for resources that I cannot find (medieval research material at the Grade 4 reading level was a tough one) and I share what I have in return.

My junior music binder has grown over the years and I have the luxury of picking and choosing the materials that I will use each year. Try to implement different exercise sheets and vary your lesson plans each year to avoid becoming tedious and repetitive. There's nothing worse than becoming as bored as your students will be after you have repeated your program more than twice in succession. With new material comes a new and fresh outlook. The facts don't change but the methods of presenting them certainly can.

For a few years, I tried to collect all of the music notebooks at the end of each school year in order to keep a flow of the history of music being taught from Grade 4 to Grade 8. In September, I handed out the books and we would continue on. This enabled most of the children to continue to compile music vocabulary words and they did not have to rewrite their notes from year to year. There is a glitch, of course, because there are always children who are new to the school and need to "catch up" AND there are always the students who lose their notebook and cannot hand it in at the year end. In September, I search for a great notebook, photocopy its contents and hand them out to these children in order to provide an accurate, neat beginning and an equal chance of continuing the program in a continuous flow like the others. There really is no point in punishing them for losing their book because it's a "done deal" and making them rewrite it causes anger and hostility, two things that you want to avoid, especially in the music program.

Children appreciate any breaks that you give them and sometimes, when you treat them well, they become the class helper and "book hander-outer", a wonderful addition to any music class.

It seems a very startling but real statistic to read that "difficult kids" often become some of your best volunteers and helpers. If you can show them that you are truly there to help them, they tend to be much more cooperative and helpful in the classroom.

ALWAYS BE FAIR TO EACH SUBJECT

Each subject area requires a long range plan and it should take its place at the front of the designated subject binder. In the case where a Board designated binder is available for the entire subject area, (Grade 7 Geography program for example) your work is done. It is your working binder and you don't have to worry about planning. Just jot down the pages that you will be working on into the correct "box" of your daybook.

When you have your long range plans completed, the rest falls into place. You break things down into months, weeks and then days. Your daybook gets penciled in for **targeted** due dates of projects and major assignments. Remember - Always remain flexible and know that dates will change. The greatest headaches attack those who are not willing to "go with the flow". You can't fight changes in the schedule so be prepared to smile and compromise; for your own sanity.

Plan for yourself

Create a long term or yearly goal for yourself - a personal plan.
Examples:

(1) plan to attend at least two math workshops this year to motivate yourself and gain new ideas

(2) search out any new computer programs that could be suitable for your classroom or any computer courses that may be available

(3) choose one or two students who are presenting a serious challenge or who are facing challenges and make them your special project. Find inspiring and unique ways to help them achieve greater successes in your class.

(4) plan a special event that will build spirit in the school and build your skills as well. A good example would be a fashion show, a talent show, or even a school trip. Choose something where teachers and students can build relationships on different levels than those in the classroom.

Supervision for Growth is a mandated part of personal development and you would be wise to have something prepared when you sit with your principal to decide an important area to concentrate on. Some principals however, do target a specific topic in each division of the school or even school wide, so be prepared for that possibility as well. This is a process where you meet with your principal to target a particular area of interest to be developed and which should be fairly personal to you. It has a time line which should be met and criteria which are monitored and recorded by you for discussion and review at a later date.

Courses and workshops keep you fresh and build your professional development while the everyday challenges build your personal success as a teacher.

Get into the swing of being a planner. While you are mastering these things, your students will begin following your example more readily.

My classroom always dedicates one bulletin board to a very large, monthly calendar. It is surrounded by pictures, illustrations or photos relating to the month and to the theme. (Example: November is Mystery Month) Students create mystery items, pictures and bring in photos relating to the topic. They can be colored, cut out of magazines or even three-dimensional. They are pinned around the calendar and even pasted on to special days or events.

Example: aliens, fossils, forensic tools, weapons, footsteps, question marks, etc.

The title above the calendar reads "MYSTERY" and students become very aware of assignment due dates as they are scheduled on the calendar with drops of blood.

Students chose this method to remind them of crucial dates and I went with it. **As gory as it may seem, most assignments were in on time** and were as creative as they could get. In other words, when the planning is creative, the juices flow, children become more comfortable and the results are simply amazing.

HAVING A GOOD IDEA IS NICE BUT SETTING A GOAL AND A DEFINITE OBJECTIVE IS KEY. IMPLEMENTING IT IN A GOOD PLAN IS VITAL.

THE DAYBOOK

Although a crucial and necessary tool, do not misunderstand the role of the daybook in your classroom. **A daybook should not contain rewritten lesson plans**. It should be a reference guide, like an index of a textbook. It should be concise, factual, and informative.

If you are a primary teacher with no rotary subjects, it should clearly state your intentions for time allotted periods throughout the day. As you must realize, the daybook is not only your tool of reference, it becomes a school document which can be perused by a principal or other educational administrator as well as a supply teacher who may be called in during an emergency or an illness.

If you are a teacher who has a homeroom as well as rotary classes, each time period should include which class is coming in and the lesson planned for that class. Again, it should make reference to a lesson plan that is detailed and clearly defined and can easily be found in the binder allotted for that subject.

The most important thing to remember is that your daybook should always be up-to-date and completed for at least one week or one cycle **ahead** of time. Even though this sounds like an enormous task, it is actually one of the easiest. Let me explain.

You have to sit down and organize your schedule on a regular basis. The easiest way to do this is to put your daybook outline in front of you when you begin. Have the shells or outline sheets photocopied for the entire term and in a binder. There are many ways to set up the pages of your daybook and that becomes a personal issue. There are a multitude of "daybook sample books" containing reproducible pages. These are found in book stores and teacher specialty shops. Even though there are many wonderful ideas out there, you may find that one or two things on the page do not suit you. Adjust the most suitable daybook outline for yourself. Be sure to keep the "master page" free of any unnecessary information as you will be using it to photocopy the year's pages.

I have found that each year, my daybook outline needs a few minor adjustments but is generally formatted to my personal needs. It is definitely a personal thing and no one can provide you with the "perfect page". Perhaps you think that I'm going on a bit too much about this. You will be reading your daybook each and every day of your teaching life. Hone it to perfection! If something isn't right, it will make you crazy each time you look at it and you have enough factors trying to "make you crazy" already. Agreed?

I am only using my personal favourite page as an example of what I have found to be effective FOR ME. It will give you some direction, but, ultimately, the choice is yours!

MY PERSONAL FAVORITE

My favorite is to turn a blank page sideways and put the days of the cycle (we had six) across top. The periods of the day are written down the side. (I use one page for the morning and the opposite page for the afternoon.) The binder is open sideways to give me a full view of the entire cycle at a moment's glance. I like to be aware of the "whole picture" rather than just one day at a time. It helps me to plan more quickly and allows for "compromising with knowledge."

Example: this is an afternoon page. I fill in a lot more information but this is the shell in order for you to get the idea.

0 my pages are on the side 0 these are the holes in the page 0

Day 1 Mon. May 3	Day 2 Tues. 4	Day 3 Wed. 5	Day 4 Thurs. 6	Day 5 Fri. 7	Day 6 Mon. 10
1:00 Gr. 4 4/4 time pg.6	Gr. 6 oral 2 part MusicCanada pg. 4-8	Gr. 4 /5 4/4 time	Gr. 4 MusicCanada pg.6	assembly	**Spare** daybook for next week
1:40 Gr. **5/6** oral music folder	Gr. 4 oral folder	Gr.5/6 oral folder	Gr. 6 staff game pg. 12	Gr. **4/5** oral folder	Gr.4/5 oral folder
2:20 **recess**	**recess**	***yard duty**	**recess**	**recess**	***yard duty**
2:35 **Homeroom** Sil. Read.	**HR** homework catch up	**HR** journal	**HR** sil. read.	**Spare**	**HR** journal
volleyball 4:00-5:00	staff mtg.		dentist 4:30		pick up Rebecca

My morning pages have a lot more information as I add the vocabulary word for each day, any prominent announcements to be reviewed or any special activities that my children may be part of. My student of the week is listed on the Monday page, etc.

The words and numbers in bold are constants on my pages. They are part of the daybook page and do not need to be filled in each cycle. I only print in the plans I have for each class. Because I am a little anal about neatness, I tend to rip out and redo any pages that get too "disturbed" so that my book always looks neat. A little too much information for you, I suppose.

The shell is the page and I print everything in myself. There is ample room in each box for the day's activities and I write extra notes at the top for special events or other important messages. Again, to reiterate, I use a full page for each half of the six day cycle giving me a lot of space to write and plan.

As I go through the weekly plan, I decide what I wish to accomplish and in what period of time. I then look at the number of periods available in the cycle, check to see if there will be any interruptions and schedule those in first. (Assemblies, guest speakers, spirit awards, sports events, etc.)

The last principal I worked with always printed out a weekly memo providing an accurate account of the upcoming week's events. There will often be minor disruptions but the memo provides a very good summary of the expectations for the week. It reports assemblies, special presentations, workshops where some staff may be absent from school (learning resource teacher), staff meetings and any other pertinent information relevant to planning time. If your school office has not put that practice into place, I would strongly suggest implementing it as soon as possible. It is a great help to staff planning!

Slowly, I create a timetable for each class in each subject area.

If I am integrating two subjects, I create a lot more flexibility for myself and play with all of the periods designated for those two classes.

Slot in any possible library periods or any extras that you can get during a research project. This is where you can provide more advantages for yourself. If you know that there will be a major assignment in November, go to the librarian and schedule a block of extra library classes for research. When it comes time for that project, you're in! No worries and no headaches. If people want to bargain for time, you have the upper hand and may get other benefits from giving up a couple of those periods. It's a game of strategy and if you play it well, you will always achieve your goals.

Block in your "spare" time and **write out** what you intend to accomplish during that time. Try to stick to your plan even though there are many distractions during those times. If you wish to call parents, write down the names of those you are going to contact. If you are planning to update your privacy binder, sit down and do it! When another staff member invites you to sit and chat about a student, set up an appointment time in order to maintain control of your spare time. You don't get much of it. Use it to your advantage and use it wisely!

I often plan my daybook during my spare periods because I can use these short blocks of time to arrange a whole cycle. Nothing feels better than going home at the end of a day knowing that you have a completed, up-to-date daybook lying on your desk, just in case!

"A productive habit is nothing more than small, consistent actions that add up to big, positive results."
Burke Hedges

IT CAN BE A NIGHTMARE!

I cannot begin to tell you the horror stories of the "sick" (I use that term loosely) teachers who feel the need to drag themselves in to school at 6:30 a.m. to complete their daybook for the supply teacher who will arrive at 8:00 a.m. to cover their class. They've been up all night wrapped around the porcelain throne and then had to call in sick to continue the battle against the flu bug. Unfortunately, they have not prepared for the day and don't wish to have an unprepared daybook sitting on their desk.

Then there are the teachers who take the daybook home to plan. It lies helpless on the dining room table while the frustrated (never to return to that class) supply teacher is left to frantically pull things together on his/her own at 8:00 a.m.

There are supply teachers who meet with empty day book pages and flip back to the last cycle to find out which group is coming to their classroom and what subject they may be teaching them.

Supply teachers are your friends and should be treated well.

Word gets around quickly and if you are an "unprepared daybook person", you may not have the luxury of a reliable teacher to fill your shoes. They have their set of standards as well and they can be your best advocate if you are prepared. Often, you have the opportunity of choosing your supply so you want to build solid bridges in order to keep your program going.

Having been a music teacher, it quickly became quite evident that good supply music teachers are harder to come by. When you do happen to get a good one, give him/her a good reason to want to keep coming back to your classroom and you will be much happier with the results. Being prepared benefits not only the supply teacher, but it also "covers your b——."

Years ago, I had a supply teacher come in and allow my students to watch soap operas all afternoon. These ingenious individuals had convinced her that we were studying soap opera plots in English class. My daybook was resting comfortably in the middle of my desk and she hadn't even bothered to read it.

I was a very young teacher at the time with an older principal who hadn't been too keen on having a twenty-two year old "slam dunked" into his school. From the beginning, he had been on a mission to provide me with a great deal of direction as to what was appropriate in his facility.

On hearing about this incident from one of his sources, I suppose he felt the need to grab yet another opportunity to storm into my room to reprimand me. As he opened his mouth to speak, I just pointed to my completed daybook and said, "It is right here, in plain view, completed to next week." He sheepishly left the room with the realization that he would have to vent elsewhere. It was during this pivotal moment that I learned about the beauty of being prepared.

CHAPTER TEN
Mistakes, I'll Make a Few

Speaking with new teachers, I often hear the phrase "**What if I make a mistake?**" I have two comeback answers to this question?

The first is "**You will.**"

The second is "**When** you make a mistake, learn from it, become a better person for it and understand that it is part of the natural process of learning."

Now, I'm not saying that you should duct-tape a talkative child's mouth shut and then plead your case as having made a mistake. Somewhere in this world it's been done and you can learn from that teacher's mistake. That poor individual is probably picking fruit somewhere and wishing they had not used Red Green's method of solving every problem with duct tape.

There must be a genuine thought process before executing the plan. What I am saying is that you have to try new ideas, lessons and projects before you give them your stamp of approval. **Don't be afraid to try!** Remember - "Triumph begins with Try." If it doesn't work out, the worst that can happen is that you apologize to your students and allow them to realize that you are a member of the human race.

My students have always been privy to the fact that math and science have never been my strong suits.

The fact is; I was given a passing mark in Grade 10 mathematics on the promise of not taking math again in Grade 11. There was some discussion about my professor's best friend teaching the Grade 11 math program and not wanting to ruin a good friendship. Anyway, being an "artsy" sixteen year old, I didn't mind at the time and ended up being tutored at a later date upon entering university.

Science, although attempted with great fervor and vigor, was just not something I could understand. Experiments looked good on paper, sounded easy enough to execute, but, after setting my Science teacher on fire (who knew how quickly sulphur could ignite), it was decided that I really didn't need Science to graduate, so there you have it.

Students need to know that you are not perfect and that you don't expect perfection. The classroom should be a comfortable place, filled with humor and acceptance.

"You made a mistake? Welcome to the club!"

I often have discussions where my teenage students openly share their embarrassing moments with the class. (This is only for those who wish to share and I have never had a student "cross the line" of appropriateness) I add a few of my own anecdotes and watch the walls of fear and anxiety disappear. I'm sure that this topic can easily be discussed at the junior level as well.

> *"PRACTICE LOVING YOURSELF, OTHERS AND LIFE IN THIS MOMENT, WITHOUT CONDITIONS".*
>
> Don Wolfe

COURAGE - PLUS!!

There is a favorite story that I like to tell my intermediate students who are so conscious of being embarrassed. (especially of that minute zit that can hardly be seen by the naked eye)

As I was nearing the end of Grade 12, I accompanied a friend of mine to the Graduation ceremonies at his high school. As each of the graduates went up to receive their diploma I, and most of those seated in the gymnasium, noticed that one of the girls had the hem of her floor-length gown tucked neatly into the back of her pantyhose. I was sure that she was unaware of this fashion statement but I, like the rest of the audience, laughed at the sight. (I'm not sure why we choose to laugh at the misfortunes of others, but it seems to be a common human characteristic. Maybe we just feel so elated that it's not our embarrassing moment that we laugh with relief).

Anyway, this unfortunate girl soon caught the gist of something being terribly amiss and, checking her backside realized, in utter horror, what had happened.

Let it be known that this is every girl's nightmare. We've all dreamt of a moment like this and woke up in a clammy sweat, grateful that we are cocooned alone in a bed with no audience to share that horriblest of dreams. (I don't know if horriblest is a real word but it seems to fit here) She slunk quickly down the stairs of the stage and I thought that we would never see her again.

95

WRONG!

This young lady reappeared a few minutes later to present her valedictory address. With surprising confidence and a grin from ear to ear, she openly checked her dress and began, "I faced quite a challenge in deciding how to capture your attention this evening. I guess my strategy worked."

I sat there in stunned disbelief as this very confident, attractive girl gave one of the most inspiring speeches that I have ever heard. She won me over as a permanent believer that there is life after embarrassment.

I tell this story to my students each year because I really learned a lot from this girl at a very impressionable age in my life and I believe that she deserves to be an example to this day by virtue of her ability to handle a difficult situation so gracefully. I'm sure that she must be running a small country somewhere.

Make your classroom a safe place where children can raise their hands to offer an answer even when they're not totally sure of its being correct.

Children are much more comfortable attempting new things in an environment that will not make fun of them if they fail.

It's always fun to share the stories of "the great failures of all time" - Walt Disney, Thomas Edison, the founder of McDonald's and many other great men who experienced a great deal of failure before achieving success. The book "You, Inc." written by Burke Hedges contains wonderful examples for you to share with your students. They are short and poignant and can be popped into lessons easily. Your students should never be afraid to make a mistake. There are SO many ways to correct them.

"Good beginning - does anyone else have anything to add to that?"

"That's an interesting thought. Anyone else?"

"Okay, I hadn't actually looked at it that way."

"That's a very unique way of looking at it. Can someone think of another approach to that question?" Try not to embarrass, always encourage and never tolerate **embarrassing** laughter.

Try to instill the importance of "laughing **with** someone, rather than **at** someone."

I have actually lain in bed some nights thinking of unique and tactful ways to tell children that their answers are not exactly right. It can be an interesting exercise, especially if you start to recognize phrases that have been used on you in the past.

I have also spent many interesting guidance lessons creating embarrassing situations for children to deal with. They include the effects and ongoing ramifications of laughing at other people's mistakes. This is never tolerated in my class.

Sometimes I can actually say, "Whoa - what were you thinking?" and get away with it because the class has understood and become very aware of the natural process of making mistakes.

I like to get my Grade 8 class to a point where they can actually listen to their own answer and realize that this one just didn't make it.

(If they can actually laugh at their own mistakes - Bonus!)

Of course, it is often made easier by the fact that I teach Science and mistakes run rampant in my lessons and experiments.

Don't be afraid to own up to your own mistakes!

While teaching Science to my unfortunate Class of 1999, I stood in front of my 42 Grade 8 students and admitted,

"I have read three chapters on this experiment, I have all of the materials in front of me and I've followed the diagrams to the letter. IT DOESN'T WORK."

During this moment of total frustration, an incredibly gifted, insightful student came forward and, in a split second, moved 2 of my "scientific" items a fraction of an inch.

VOILA! The gasses began to form.

Andrew B. and I team taught for the rest of the year and I paid him well (pizza and chocolate). We still keep in touch and I will always be grateful to this impressive young man who taught me a great deal about Science and being true to myself.

Not knowing the age group that you will be teaching or how comfortable you are in allowing scraps of your personal life to enter the classroom, I ask you to judge this next section for yourself.

As the years have gone by, I have become more open and honest with my students. I have shared tragic moments and humorous anecdotes quite freely as the opportunities arose. I'm getting older now and I have a lot less to lose. My students have become like my own children and if I feel they can benefit from a mistake that I have made, then I put it out there for their learning.

I genuinely love "my kids" and most of the times that I have truly connected with them, it was during a personal moment. (also on those less formal school trips where I can truly be myself and do the Kool-Aid dyeing hair thing - another story, another time)

If my experiences can teach them, then so be it. I have understood for many years now that I no longer have to defend my past errors. I have had to learn and grow from them just as everyone else does. If they can be used to improve my life, then perhaps they can help to improve the lives of others.

In true fact, one of my greatest personal challenges prompted me to become a teacher and I work hard to instill in my students, the philosophy, "that out of adversity comes opportunity". My goal has been to teach this valuable lesson early in life unlike waiting the length of time it took for me to realize it.

I enjoy reading the collection of contemplative essays compiled by **Joanne D'Alton Clancy**. She has written a book of *ideas*, sometimes poignant and always spirited. Many words deal with the important issues addressed in this book so I have taken the liberty of sharing some of them with you. Her book is aptly named "a way out from in".

"GREATNESS"

"All great men have not always had great thoughts. Step by step, like children in a dark corridor, they have had to learn to differentiate the light from the darkness.

Their greatness, in many instances, has grown through the overcoming of their own inadequacies, and in realizing that the pages of time are not completely written at this moment, but through many moments to come.

They, like the rest of us, have made mistakes but they learn and profit by these same mistakes. However that may be, each one of us during our life, at one time or another, is given a moment wherein we, too, can touch the height of greatness.

You don't have to be famous to be a great man - your greatness speaks for itself in the little things which you do in your daily life."

Joanne D'Alton Clancy

How dare we judge a child by their mistakes AND how dare we carry that judgement for years, not allowing them the privilege of overcoming the stigma of the flawed character we have created for them. Listen to the discussion in the staff room about a child "from 4 years ago..."

Let's all make a pact right now -

We will try to help children make less mistakes but we will allow errors to be made and show them how to use them as learning experiences.

Understand that I speak of "learning" mistakes as opposed to "manipulative behavior". You will soon come to know the difference and children should be able to clearly understand your tolerance levels. Don't allow them to even think that they can get away with manipulating your motives. They are intelligent little creatures who require clearly defined boundaries.

As I have stated a few times, children need to be in an environment where they feel comfortable enough to make mistakes. Often, it is stressful enough for them to attempt anything new, so it behooves us to lay a solid, "safe" groundwork for these honest attempts.

"I discovered at an early age that I missed 100% of the shots I did NOT take."

Wayne Gretzky

"DESIGN" Joanne D'Alton Clancy

"Life is like a patchwork quilt - the crazy pattern of the pieces to be carefully sewn together by us to make our own individual life design.

In our youth, nothing seems to jibe in this crazy quilt of ours, but as we grow older the pieces begin to slowly fit into the whole, just like a jigsaw puzzle.

As we look back over the years at some of the designs for living which we have used, we realize that, in many cases, we dropped quite a few stitches here and there!

However, it is not wise to wish one's self back for a repeat performance, as we could not take our present experience with us. All we can do is see that our quilt becomes more attractive, more harmonious with the years, and that the stitches used are the thread of our Present, woven with the strength of the Past into the tranquility of the Future."

I would like to complete this section on "Mistakes" with a very powerful poem written by Nadine Stair. I find it to be a thought provoking piece which certainly impresses the importance of "Taking Reasonable Risks" and not being so concerned about "Making Mistakes".

IF I HAD MY LIFE TO LIVE OVER

If I had my life to live over again,
I would try to make more mistakes next time.
I would relax, limber up, I would be crazier than I ever was this time
around.
I know very few things that I would take seriously anymore.
I would take more chances, take more trips.
I'd climb more mountains, I'd swim more rivers, I'd watch more
sunsets.
I'd eat more ice cream...and fewer beans.
I'd have more actual troubles and fewer imaginary ones.
For you see, I was one of those people that lived prophylactically,
sensibly, sanely, hour after hour, day after day.
Oh, I've had my moments.
And if I had it to do all over again,
I'd try to have nothing else, just moments, one, after another.
Instead of living so many years ahead of my day.
I was one of those people that never went anywhere without a hot
water bottle,
thermometer, a gargle, raincoat, and a parachute.
If I had it to do all over again,
I'd travel lighter, much lighter, than I have in the past.
I'd take my shoes off earlier in the Spring.
And stay that way later in the Fall.
I'd ride more merry-go-rounds, catch more brass rings, and greet
more people.
I'd pick more flowers and dance more often.
If I had it to do all over again,
But you see...I don't.

MOTHER EASE

While teaching at the Children's Center, I team taught with a wonderful speech pathologist who shared many of my views and values. She was an extraordinary mother and we clicked well as a team. We adopted the term "Mother Ease" in our classroom because we both felt that one of the most important components for successful learning was a comfortable, risk-free environment.

The School Age Language Program ran two classes each day, one in the morning, reaching a group of children exhibiting receptive language delays and a group in the afternoon exhibiting expressive language delays.

For the morning program, five year old children from all over the Niagara Region began arriving by bus at 8:15 a.m. and continued to arrive until approximately 8:50 a.m. During this time and until 9:15 a.m., these little ones were encouraged to interact and play together. A wide variety of toys, puzzles, legos and games were spread about the classroom allowing a Kindergarten-like atmosphere of free movement and play.

Keep in mind that many of these children were non-verbal or frightened of communicating with others. It was often quite a challenge to coax them into play with their peers. Ann and I would sit **in the middle of the room** and discuss results of meetings, evaluations and our plans for the day's activities. We spoke softly, with humor and remained as quiet as possible in order for the students to move about uninterrupted. Every once in a while, a tiny hand would reach up and tug at our clothing, a smile would meet our eyes and play would resume.

I remember one little boy in particular. He would come up to us, arms outstretched, receive his comforting hugs and, sporting a toothy grin, return to his speechless activity. Often, his wandering eyes would fix on us. He would smile, nod his head and once again return his focus to his solitary task. You could see the need for positive reinforcement and its effect when it was received.

Months later, this sweet little boy began to interact with others, offering a favorite toy or building block to another child. Speech was sporadic and often indiscernible but we were thrilled by the progress that he had made. This was the beginning. He was learning to take reasonable risks.

It was our firm belief that "Mother Ease", the process of quietly sitting and keeping watch over our little charges, allowed them to move ever so slowly and carefully out of their comfort zones to take reasonable risks. We were always there, guardians, a quiet understood support that never failed them.

Our solid friendship with each other relayed positive "vibes" and the children knew that they were safe. Hugs were given freely and it was not uncommon to have a child nestled on one of our laps for a few minutes during this time of interaction and play. We both agreed at the end of each year that the term "Mother Ease" defined the important process that we had grown up with. Our mothers had sat with their friends and neighbors in the yard, having tea, canning, knitting or crocheting, sharing recipes etc. while we children played around them, feeling their presence and knowing that we were safe. What a wonderful experience it was to make that a viable process in our classroom. Thanks, Ann!

LEARN TO INCORPORATE NEW IDEAS

I cherish the memories of these touching experiences as they enriched my life as well as the lives of these little ones. I often silently thank the team of personnel at this facility for teaching me so many valuable lessons. Mother Ease became a more integral part of my own life and I believe that my children have benefited greatly from it.

I included this because I wish to encourage those who teach Kindergarten or other young groups of children in a team teaching setting to incorporate "Mother Ease" into your classrooms. Young children need hugs and a sense of security. It is an important part of successful learning and it will give you, the teacher, an opportunity to watch them at comfortable play, to see conflicts resolved and the development of social pragmatics in these youngsters. The learning skills section of the present report card deals with the very things that go on during this time of play and teachers are one of the greatest influences in the lives of these young children. Having had the experience of working with these little ones, my respect for those who teach them has greatly increased. Your job is enormous and you deserve a great deal of credit. Hats off to you!

AN EXCERPT

I believe that children are our future.
Teach them well and lead the way.
Show them the beauty that they possess inside.
Give them a sense of pride to make it easier.
Let the children's laughter remind us how we used to be.

Taken from the song "The Greatest Love" by Michael Master and
Linda Creed

"PERFECTION"

"None of us are infallible as we go through life. Nevertheless, sometimes those errors that we make or disappointments we may have, turn out to be most fortunate for our well-being and happiness. Sounds paradoxiacal, does it not? And yet it really isn't. Consider a mistake. If discovered, attention is focused on you - either by your own inner knowledge or through others bringing it to your attention and through this, future errors can be avoided.

If life were such that we were to follow a set routine constantly with no mistakes, where would progress be? Certainly, we would be caught in the quicksand of nonentity."

Joanne D'Alton Clancy

CHAPTER ELEVEN
CLASSROOM MANAGEMENT

"We help a child create a sense of significance and value by providing a proper balance of NURTURE (unconditional love and support) and STRUCTURE (consistent guidelines with consistent and firm enforcement of agreed upon consequences)". Jack Canfield

Prior to beginning your first term in September, I challenge you to develop **"THE LOOK"**.

The LOOK should be a finely tuned facial stare that, when shot across the room, immediately causes enough anxiety to the receiving child that he/she will question his/her negative behavior and put a stop to it at once.

The LOOK, by virtue of its name, should produce intimidation and the promise of an accountable action to follow if the undesired behavior does not end immediately.

You must practice the LOOK in the mirror each morning and before you go to bed at night. It should be shot randomly at your friends, family and pets. If and when your new puppy cowers and ends his habit of wetting the carpet, you have it mastered.

When executing the LOOK, be sure that, if ignored, it is directly followed by a suitable, pre-arranged punishment. Create a list of "good punishment rules" with or without class input. Be sure that your students are informed and understand the consequences of inappropriate behaviors at the very beginning of the school year. Of course, since you are the author of all, you may change consequences each term, but always with their knowledge. No surprises - no argument!!

If you don't _____, you will have to
_____or
If you _____, you must
_____.

Be specific! Wishy-washy promises that are not kept will soon devalue your authority and you can't risk that. You have the power to fill in the blanks with a virtual plethora of consequences.

One of the more useful ways to inflict punishment is to find the weakest subject area for the student in question and assign work in that area. This allows for children to actually learn and accomplish constructive "home" work while being punished at the same time. Explain that you must give them a consequence for their negative actions but you would like it to benefit them in some way. Children often appreciate your candor and sincerity and will comply more readily. Parents appreciate this form of punishment and will often supervise and even correct the work that is completed by their child.

Although you should be a friend, children need to know that you are "The Boss"
and inappropriate behaviour will not be tolerated.

One of my favorites is **"THE PARAGRAPH".**

A creative, flowery, well-written, looooong paragraph has often become the punishment to fit the crime in my classroom.

For example: Paul has just shot a spitball into Carly's mass of curly red hair. That particular action is not acceptable in my classroom and therefore I would write on the board;

"It is important for me to realize that my very rude action can cause a wide variety of consequences. It can physically hurt someone if my shot is not accurate, it could cause a "hair nightmare" for a student and it is an extremely nausea-causing action. I don't believe that I would enjoy someone else's saliva careening through and planting itself in my hair. I will not repeat that action again because the punishment would become much more severe than merely having to write this paragraph 25 times."

The paragraphs must be written by hand and, depending upon the severity of the crime, signed by a parent upon completion. The latter part of this is the ultimate problem for most children because often they do not wish their parents to find out what they have done.

If it is a misdemeanor that I feel will not be repeated, I will sometimes "make a deal" and not require a parent's signature. It can become a trust issue rewarding both you and the child with a little bond. Of course, if this trust is broken, there will be no more deals.

Generally, parents wish to be informed of any wrongdoing so this is a way to inform but not "tattle". You don't have to call the parent at this point to complain about disruptive behaviors. They have read and signed the pages written by their child. Often, the signature is accompanied by an apology from either the parent, the child or both.

I have a great deal of respect for parents who are willing to admit that their child is still in the process of learning and making mistakes. It makes me feel part of a team, rather than a free-floating agent in this child's life. If the negative action is one that is very disturbing to the parent, an interview can be arranged and some solutions can be drawn up.

My paragraphs have become infamous. Children from miles around have heard about the dreaded paragraph and every new student is quickly oriented to the "paragraph thing." Sometimes the class will help to write the paragraph and are pleased that this time, they are not on the receiving end of the well-thought out goal on the board.

Thesauruses and dictionaries are often used to find rather unusual words and we often share a meaningful vocabulary lesson at the same time.

At the end of the year, upon reading the letters and cards that children leave on my desk, the notorious "paragraphs" are often mentioned and understood. Recipients confide that they learned a lot from them and make promises never to repeat those inappropriate actions even though they will not be in my class again. (My Grade 8s go on to high school at that point)

"Paragraphs" have become a source of both humor and dread and it is clearly understood that they are to be avoided at all costs.

Who says that all crimes must be so serious that they can't be viewed as even a little light-hearted? Often, because we deal with problems so openly, children are more willing to share their feelings, and real forgiveness takes place. I believe that this openness is often followed by true remorse. Gauge for yourself the level of seriousness and a noteworthy lesson can be learned.

It is vital that the new September class does not clearly see your warm and fuzzy side until at least six weeks into the year.

They should see a smiling, positive, enthusiastic teacher who has their best interests at heart but who will not put up with any "shenanigans". (a wonderful word that my Grade 3 teacher, Miss Barnhardt, used often)

Loving children does not mean giving them license to walk all over you. True love requires discipline, guidance and rules to protect them from themselves and each other.

During my early years, I taught in an inter-city junior high school where discipline and control are key. My first nick-name was the "Blonde Bitch" and I was devastated. I stuck to my guns, however, because a very knowledgeable teacher explained to me that I could always become nice but I could never regain "lost control".

In a couple of months, I started to add more humor and personal anecdotes to my lessons. My choirs, held after school, became more informal meetings where we took breaks and chatted. Soon, I had won not only the respect and attention of my students, but their genuine acceptance as well. My nickname disappeared, never to be heard again.

That teacher had been right! "Take the abuse at the beginning; the love will come". It did.

Each year, new students attended the school and the older ones would give them the "scoop" that I was OK. Although, that fact wasn't always accepted at the beginning, gradually it was learned and I enjoyed many successful years of teaching some very difficult students.

At another placement, I was dubbed "Atilla the Hearn", a nickname that I found rather amusing. It was a well-kept "secret" and I applaud the creativity of the person who gave it to me. One afternoon, the class, a special ed. group, asked if we could participate in a particular outing. I told them that Atilla the Hearn would not allow them to go but perhaps if they asked Mrs. Hearn, she would be willing to take them. Laughter ensued, realization that teachers are all-knowing beings struck them and that was the end of the title I had been given.

Sometimes it's just as brief and unintentional as that. The trip was fun, we had a great time and my true feelings were now allowed to spill into the classroom.

There are many cited methods of gaining and keeping control in your classroom. Here is my personal NEVER do. (Excuse my grammar but you understand my point)

NEVER YELL AT CHILDREN ON A REGULAR BASIS BECAUSE THEY WON'T HEAR YOU.

There is nothing worse than "the screamer", a teacher who loves to hear his own voice shrieking high above the constant din in the room. I don't use the words "constant din" lightly. If the teacher is a screamer, there will always be noise in the room because the students have tuned her out. Screaming is not an effective way to maintain control. I cannot emphasize that enough.

If you want the attention of your students, one of the methods is to lower your voice. Children will strain to hear you and, should they not be able to, they will "shush" the children around them. Soon the entire class is hushed and waiting to hear what you have to say. It does work if you implement this at the beginning of the year. Months of screaming and then switching to whispering will only cause you frustration because generally the class won't notice. It must become a new goal for the next class. Sorry, but that's a fact that I've witnessed.

A very sincere teacher approached me with her problem of gaining control. It seemed that, even though she yelled at the class to quiet down, the children just wouldn't listen. As we reviewed the problem, she read a handout that I had prepared on classroom management. She decided with great enthusiasm to try **the whispering technique.** Unfortunately, it fell on deaf ears.

The children were so programmed to her loud voice that they hadn't noticed her attempts to communicate with them on a quieter level. She returned to report that it had failed and she wanted to try something else. It was May and I challenged her to try again but to begin her next school year with the "whisper method". I believe that she had developed it to perfection by October and uses it very effectively to this day.

Another way to gain the attention of the class is by **flicking the lights on and off a few times**. It can become the signal for everyone to return to their seats, stop talking, clean up art supplies and so on. It is effective, causes no physical discomfort and becomes a routine that is welcomed by students at any Grade level. Theaters use it all the time to bring audiences back to their seats and I have reminded my senior students of this fact from time to time. I repeat - It is quiet, understood and effective.

Serious Crowd Control

Over the years, my choirs have consisted of 12 to 140 students. When I combine my junior and senior choirs for certain events, the number can reach 250. Drastic measures have to be taken in order to maintain control. I do ask for a teacher to come in and supervise at the back because I am not arrogant enough to think that every child will be paying attention to me and participating when I am not looking directly at them. When I wish to gain control, my hand goes up; straight up in the air for all to see. It takes approximately 5 to 10 seconds to get everyone back under control. Most schools use this method for assemblies and large audience events.

Principals can command an entire student body with one arm raised in the air. It is a wonderful thing to see. Visitors to the school sit in amazement and reach new levels of admiration as they watch a noisy gymnasium settle down in a very short time.

I remember a certain trip to Brock University. Our entire school, staff and students, has the opportunity to spend an entire morning at the Brock University pool each year. We are talking about approximately 420 wet children huddled on the bleachers, wrapped in towels, and almost flying off their seats in anticipation.

One individual must go over the rules with them and this particular year, that individual happened to be me. I put up my hand knowing that the entire group would stop talking and give me their full, undivided attention and... they did.

One of the parents, who had no idea that this was a common practice and that anyone could have done the same thing with our group, was so impressed that he reported it to everyone within a thirty-mile radius. In his opinion, I was a miracle worker.

He had no idea that any one of our staff with arms was equipped to do the same thing. It was a well-known procedure that was utilized on a regular basis. A monkey could have commanded the same response at our school but I never told him that. I like fame and so I wallowed in his praise for quite some time allowing him to think whatever he wished. It's a free world, after all.

Just last week, I had the opportunity of visiting my daughter's school. There was an assembly and the audience was given the opportunity to enjoy the beautiful voices of primary, junior and senior students in their various choirs. Their leaders (there were two) used a clapping method to get the students' full, undivided attention. Each teacher **clapped out a rhythm** and the entire choir followed her lead by repeating the rhythm. It was an interesting exercise in gaining control but it also showed their ability to repeat rhythms, a lesson that was obviously part of their curriculum and met the skills outlined in the music guide.

Another great way to keep things under control in the classroom is through the use of **the point system**. The class has a certain number of points at the beginning of the day. Each time there is a problem, a point is lost. Each point lost could represent the loss of a number of minutes of recess, an activity or a special class treat.

In other words, with the loss of a point comes the loss of a valued item. The number of minutes lost could be spent in silence during a recess time or after school depending upon the location of your school. (Bussed schools require that all children leave the premises on the bus unless parents have agreed to pick up their child)

You could start with a positive rather than build a negative depending upon what works more easily for you. You can give points throughout the day as positive things occur.

BE YOURSELF

I have always used the points system in my class because we have a mutual respect for chocolate. (I know - there are those of you who don't believe in rewards of candy - sorry! That's my personal thing and you are certainly allowed yours. One of the beauties of teaching is that it allows you to exercise your own personal preferences.)
Students earn points for
-homework completion
-a signed organizer
-good deeds (can be directed towards helping a student or staff member)
-stages of a time line completed correctly
You get the picture.
On Fridays, I put out a variety of candy worth points.

Tootsie pops	-5 points
sour keys	-3 points
small chocolate bar	-5 points
small bag of chips	-5 points and so on

Everyone is able to accumulate some points over the course of the week and we have a small snack fest at the end of the day. For students who wish to accumulate more points, there are greater prizes. Points "cap out" at a certain level and must be "cashed in". We have gone to the movies, out for lunch and taken weekend bike hikes for "major point accumulation."

This point system has always been my personal favorite because children love rewards and they love to be recognized. It is a little more work and can become somewhat costly so I don't recommend it to everyone. I use it as an example of positive reinforcement that has been very successful for me over the course of many years because it generally motivates children to avoid bad behaviors. It greatly reduces the need for punishment which is a goal for me. I must admit that I have been criticized from time to time about rewarding children for good behaviours and "bribing" them. It seems to me that there would be a lot fewer people in the work force if there was no pay check at the end of a week. Just my thought!

These strategies are a just a few ideas for you to try . Meaningful workshops lead by talented people in your Boards are constantly provided and it behooves you to sign up and learn.

They deal with many of these and other issues. When it comes to learning, you are never alone. Call the Board office, express your concerns and they will put you in touch with the people who can guide you to solutions. Unfortunately, the days of plentiful superintendents are over but there are still many good people struggling to fulfill the wishes of Board employees and I have great respect for their efforts.

Trips

While we are on the subject of management, I would like to address the issue of trips. Your Board or principal will have a list of places that has been deemed appropriate for school trips and it is always a pleasure to take a group of curious children on an outing. Choose destinations that will be both interesting and educational, a difficult combination to achieve, but, with proper planning, a feat that can be accomplished successfully.

Trips, as you have probably surmised, play a diversity of roles in the lives of your students. They provide educational experiences and that is what you tell all of those inquisitive parents who have a need to justify everything that their child participates in. Trips then blossom out and bloom much further. Any group of children being plopped into a strange setting away from the rules and eyes of the entire school staff tend to show their "true" colors. Many of them will surprise you with their innate sense of right and wrong, their ability to display well taught manners and their positive social skills. Others will act exactly the way you expected them to when it comes to showing off and performing for strangers in an unfamiliar setting. They will require constant supervision and the full expectation that they will be reprimanded for any disruptions that they cause. Then there are the children who "don't get out much" and truly are at a loss as to what is expected of them. They seldom visit restaurants or touring facilities, they have probably never stayed in a hotel or university dorm and they really don't know how to behave. This is the group that you have the opportunity to really impact. A few pointers here and there, some reminders or examples of good behaviors and a lot of encouragement when positive changes occur cause these children to reap a multitude of learning skills. Hopefully, they get to see your "silly side" as you reinforce your expectations, fully realizing that your expectations are high. Always aim high and expect the best from your students BUT be prepared for some disappointing results. It's a fact and not to be taken personally.

LIGHTEN UP

Let me give you an example:

While visiting a museum, one of my talkative students wouldn't let up on private whispering in the corner. I put my arm around his shoulder and "took him for a walk" explaining the difficulties of being a tour guide and how they deserve much more money than what they are paid for what they do. "It wouldn't seem fair to make their job more of a burden because someone was disrespectful enough to talk during their presentation. Let's try to understand how much they have to remember as they spew facts out for the benefit of their audience."

Upon returning the student to his spot, I noticed one of the younger male teachers chatting to another teacher in the corner. I immediately went over, put my arm around his shoulder and took him for the same walk. It was done in such a way that the student "got it" and the teacher was able to smile and understand what I had done. We can be light-hearted but give a serious message. Fortunately, this lesson was learned and we all noticed an improvement in appropriate behaviours when listening to the guides.

I would like to look at day trips and overnight trips separately because they are distinctly different and you must prepare carefully for both.

Read and remember my chapter on **The Parent Trap** before you choose parents as volunteer chaperones. A good selection of parent volunteers can create a successful trip while one difficult parent can cause that same trip to be "hellish". Choose carefully. There are always criteria that can be set to eliminate those parents who can be slotted into the "unfit" category.

- two volunteers have already sent their notes in prior to your note coming in

(Keep "blanket" notes of solid volunteers in your desk for future trips)

-we are asking for only male parents this time (or female)

-we have enough teachers to support the number of students

-we would like to give other parents a chance

-we have set a limit of one parent per year in order to accommodate all of the volunteers

If you don't have many volunteers from your class, then you can ask parents from other classes in order for the children to "have more independence". You are creative and intelligent. You can come up with a very acceptable reason for this particular parent not to fit the criteria.

To ensure that you have parents "on board", go over a few stringent rules with them at the outset. Explain that their presence is required during the **entire** trip (evenings included) in order to insure that they don't go off for a break when you need them the most. Many times, I have seen volunteers head out to dinner leaving me and the principal with a group of eighty children eating at the designated restaurant. Children eat quickly! You too, are tired, and are now left to handle the excited masses who are trying every trick in the book to escape. Explain the seriousness of rules that will assure you of quality care and control! Give your assistants appropriate responsibilities and expect them to follow through.

Whenever you can find a field trip that provides educational materials, it's a bonus. It helps you to build your resources and you know that the information has been well researched. Generally speaking, the guides will "know their stuff" and you can pretty much rely on an educated, informed staff at that location. Much of the review and discussion work has been done for you so "why re-invent the wheel?"

Day trips can include:

(1) a local zoo filled with not only a variety of animals but booklets and handouts to be used as reference and review materials.

(2) a conservation area with "informative, organized" guides who will take your students on an adventure as they study plant and mineral life.
We took a group of intermediate students to our local area called "Woodend" to complete a photography unit. Students were organized into small groups, each of which received a disposable camera and a full set of instructions. Each picture taken had to fill a certain criteria. There was a great deal of fun, laughter and an amazing array of beautifully developed pictures which were later arranged into promotional "Woodend" advertisement collages for the school. Often, barbecues or other fun lunches can be arranged at the site for the enjoyment of your group. Conservation areas are great for scavenger hunts and creating science booklets. Be sure to prepare your students with the required information before visiting your chosen site.

(3) a trip to a science center where children have the opportunity to roam independently and participate in experiments, physical fitness activities or even view live coverage of the

115

space station. Children love the idea of freedom and these facilities provide a great deal of it in a very secure setting. Clearly designated personnel are scattered throughout the facility to answer questions, give directions and reunite that "lost" student with their group.

(4) an art gallery that is age appropriate and interesting. Hands on galleries where children may actively participate in creating a masterpiece of their own is suggested. An art gallery idea sounds good at the time but if you don't check carefully, it can become a boring and unmanageable environment, especially for the younger ones.

(5) any interactive museum, historical fort or sites where children are invited to be involved and busy. There are usually a series of workshops available and children can participate in a range of activities from wearing uniforms and studying weapons to making music or cooking basic food recipes.

Always look for places where children can move, interact, ask questions, get involved or even leave with a finished piece of art work. Trips should be a fun place where teaching continues without a "school" setting.

You may work on particular goals but always keep in mind that pragmatics are an integral part of the teaching process. Learning to use correct manners and appropriate behaviors, practicing good moral conduct, displaying respectful habits such as removing hats indoors and no gum chewing are all part of the experience on trips. A "biggie" that needs constant reinforcement is "learning to ask appropriate questions." Often, children ask guides how old they are, if they're married or other personal issues. They seem to feel that these questions are valid but we know that they are not. Students must learn that the private lives of tour guides and personnel are not topics for discussion and should be reminded of this continuously. Eventually, hopefully, it will become natural for them to respect the privacy of others and move on to more relevant questioning.

We tend to become a little more lax with the children when we travel with them and that is fine, but be sure to maintain a high code of conduct and enforce it throughout the trip. If you don't, you will slowly lose control and things can get out of hand very quickly. Some teachers believe that they have to act more like "the kids" when they are out. Again, that's fine - as long as all of "the kids" remain respectful and follow the guidelines set out for appropriate behaviors. An element of respect and authority must be evident at all times - NO MATTER WHAT!

OVERNIGHT TRIPS

When arranging for a group of students to travel on overnight excursions, you can now rely on professionals to do the work for you. There are many good tour groups that will organize your trip to suit the needs of your students. When choosing the tour company, check the following carefully.

(1) How many trips does this company take children at your division level on per year? (Junior, intermediate, senior) If you are satisfied that they supervise a good number of trips, you can become more confident in their knowledge and ability to coordinate a meaningful itinerary.

(2) Does the agenda include **relevant** visits and experiences for your students. In other words, will they be visiting sites that are interesting for their age and curriculum expectations.

(3) Are the time allotments for each activity realistic?
Don't have your students running from one activity or place to another. They need breathing space and a little time to relax. If there is a shopping area in the vicinity, fit it into the middle of a hectic day in order for the kids to "chill out" a bit. They should be given ample time to eat their meals as well as an alternative place to sit and socialize if they finish early. (My experience is that a child can wolf down an entire meal in the time it takes for his/her friend to order theirs) When feeding sixty children, many are finished while others haven't even started. Entertainment during a meal or a rest area away from the eating clientele is a great idea if it can be done. If you are in a shopping mall, free time can begin right after they eat.

117

(4) Make sure that there is at least one game-oriented event that children can enjoy. Don't make everything totally educational and "by the book". There are games and activities that children can enjoy which may not fit the academic criteria of your curriculum but will enhance good sports etiquette or other learning tools. Example: paint balling, bicycle tours, or even a dance where another school group has been invited. Generally, students appreciate this "little extra" and tend to be more supportive and well-behaved when entering a quiet, more educational setting.

(3) Do the sleeping accommodations suit the group? This is a huge question and should be worked out carefully. When taking a group of intermediate students anywhere overnight, there are many factors to keep in mind.

a) Decide on the number of students per room and allow them to choose their own roommates (within reason, of course) This allows for less bickering and, if it doesn't work out, it's not your fault!

b) try to provide a party room or a central meeting place for all of your students to meet at the end of the day until 10:00 p.m. It gives them a chance to review the day and wind down a bit. If you wish to serve refreshments, avoid sugars and caffeine products. Go for juice, milk, chips, pizza and things that will help them to relax and calm down rather than rev up. You can always tell the teachers who have never given birth or had the experience of fatherhood because they hand out Mars bars at the 10:30 room check to "help kids calm down". Yes, you Beth!

c) Set a definite time that you expect them to be in their rooms. I set 10:00 p.m. in their own room and 10:30 p.m. for lights out. I enforce this rule very strictly. We all know that this won't actually happen right on schedule but it gets the ball rolling a little more quickly and generally by midnight, things are fairly quiet. If kids are allowed to choose their own roommates, they tend not to argue as much about returning to their rooms because they still have their "best" friends to socialize with. You can make the last night an exception and extend their evening activity to 11:00 p.m. It could give you leverage for more positive results during the previous night's curfew.

d) Be sure that the tour company provides security guards for the night . They should arrive a few minutes before 11:00 p.m. This is an extremely important feature as teachers and chaperones need their sleep just as much as the students do. It's also a good idea for the teachers and chaperones to "camp out" in the halls until the security guard/s arrive in order for students to realize that there will be no allowances made for roaming. Also, I've learned that the ice machine has a certain magnetic attraction to kids after 10:00 so I encourage them to "fill up" before then and to avoid filling wastebaskets. Their ice buckets provide plenty of ice for the night. We can only guess what they plan on doing with all that ice anyway.

Years ago, (in the dinosaur age of teaching) when we had to organize our own trips, staff had to stay up all night monitoring the "rovers" and the adventurous "window climbers in search of excitement or a girl's phone number". It became a proven fact that a lack of sleep left much room for carelessness and by the time chaperones were ready to go home, they were totally exhausted and could hardly handle the noise levels on the bus. When teachers are well rested, that can be a nice time to chat and socialize.

e) Respect the bus driver and ask the children to help you maintain a comfortable noise level while traveling. The driver has a great responsibility in getting you safely to your destination. The added strain of sudden outbursts, screaming or even loud chanting and singing for long periods of time can seriously jeopardize that safety. Even though they try adjust to sound levels, it still requires staff intervention to keep those levels at a reasonable place.

f) set definite but reasonable guidelines for the consequences of inappropriate actions and **stick to them**. If you have told a student that they will be sent home if..., then you must send them home if they commit the crime **SO** set feasible, realistic consequences and don't punish yourself. In other words, when students are told that they will not be allowed to participate in a certain fun activity if they break a rule, then be prepared to spend that designated time with the student who breaks the rule. You must follow through on your promises or "you are toast".

Make all consequences realistic and not "over the top". Remember that many of these children "don't get out much" and may not always know how to handle themselves appropriately. Be prepared to make allowances and don't be too quick to promise punishment that may be too harsh. Some children make great strides in learning on these trips and we have to try to help them by understanding the process that they are going through. Often, that learning takes place through your patience and understanding so "take it easy on them" and try to understand where they are coming from.

You have the power to control a lot of factors on these trips. Assigning students to certain groups and giving them a particular leader are two ways in which to separate troublemakers. Making partners accountable for each other's behavior is not always fair to the student who is "good" so keep the leader in charge of appropriate behaviors. Set rules of conduct while preparing for the trip and reinforce these rules each time you are together on the bus.

g) When traveling by bus for long distances, a video machine is often used to help "to entertain the troops". Be sure to choose the videos yourself and peruse them before you go. It is very difficult to remember every scene of a movie that you watched a few years ago and thought was "acceptable". I have had the distinct pleasure of putting in a movie and watching in horror as the breast of a beautiful young girl was exposed during a windstorm. Silly me, I had forgotten that small detail because I had been a grown-up who didn't react to these things like pubescent grade eight boys do. And, do you remember Simon Birch, that innocent, children's movie? Think again. I reiterate. PREVIEW ALL MOVIES THAT YOU PLAN TO SHOW DURING THE TRIP. You will relax, the parents will trust you more, and the children will inevitably be thrilled to have a movie to watch on the bus. I sometimes get groans and ask, "Would you like to watch The Hunchback of Notre Dame or a blank screen?" They catch my drift and we sit back to enjoy the Disney feature that I deemed appropriate. If the noise levels on the bus rise and they don't wish to watch, off it goes, only to be tried again at a later time in the trip.

h) Keep an open mind and a positive attitude when traveling with children. This is not a holiday for you, it is a teaching experience and you have to wrap yourself around that fact. Everything you do and say revolves around your charges and will be taken home. Tread carefully and positively, smiling as much as you can and reinforcing the fact that these kids have the best teachers in the world and you've made the trip to prove it.

CHAPTER TWELVE
WE'LL HAVE FUN! FUN! FUN!

I have often heard it said that kids today just want to have fun and that it can't always be fun in the classroom. I guess we would have to look at the meaning of the word "fun".

A couple of years ago, I made my way through a Science classroom with great envy as I watched a very intriguing lesson (all Science teachers should be applauded) being taught by a mesmerizing teacher who involved her students in such a way that they were on the edge of their seats waiting to hear the outcome of the experiment and the completion point of the lesson. They were having fun!

I have walked into a "manipulatives" math class where children were recording their findings in individual math journals and comparing their data with that of their fellow classmates. I have seen incredible lego machines and buildings being measured and graphed. There was fun!

My Grade 8s have re-enacted historical moments, dramatized Scrooge and his Spirits, depicted visual images of poetry they created and climbed the Alps to discover the Iceman of the Bronze Age. We have had fun!

BRINGING DRAMA INTO THE CLASSROOM

I remember a particular passage from Dickens' "A Christmas Story." As I may have mentioned, I love to read and instill this in my students. Some children have difficulty reading normal, present-day books so Dickens becomes quite a challenge. Even so, I have a need to teach about the life and works of Charles Dickens because he was such a great example of the capabilities of a poor, young author who became a literary icon. How many versions of "A Christmas Story" are there to this date? I have lost track. Again, I digress.

The classroom was dark, the curtains pulled, the flashlights subdued (I used to use candles but I learned that the fire department frowns upon that and so we use flashlights) and the students were dressed in their innovative costumes.

121

One of my very poor readers had begged to play the role of Scrooge for this chapter and so there he was, dressed in a navy terry cloth bathrobe, hair greased and flying about his shoulders, book in hand and ready to meet the Spirit of the Future.

I felt that, because things looked pretty bleak for old Scrooge, some stuttering during his journey would probably have been appropriate anyway.

This boy had been given two nights to practice his lines for the chapter and I held my breath in hopes that he would not be humiliated when reading orally in front of the group. As the Spirit of the Future entered the room, "Scrooge" began.

If you are familiar with the story, you will know that this particular Spirit does not speak. The lines are up to Scrooge and he asks all of the questions, comes up with the answers and realizes his own fate. Only the stretched out bony finger of Death cues him.

This young boy never once looked down at the book in front of him. He began to recite Scrooge's lines in a clear, agitated voice, expressing sincere concern for his future. He didn't miss a word on the page and not once did he falter. He had memorized the entire chapter and played the part well enough to audition for the next showing of the play. I was totally taken aback and then came that thought.

"You didn't have enough faith in him. How can you instill faith in your students if you don't have faith in them to begin with?"

Another mistake! I was so busy worrying about the possibility of error that I didn't give him the credit that he deserved.

Do students always do well when given an assignment they desire? Of course not; but they do deserve the benefit of the doubt. I began to relax and thoroughly enjoy the rest of the play.

Remember - it's all about having fun!

If this actor would have bogged down, then I would have had to deal with it. Don't spend time worrying until you have to accommodate or change a situation. Then, deal with it because you are a professional who can.

One of the qualities that brought you to teaching is the ability to compromise and "go with the flow". If that statement doesn't fit your profile, make it fit!

Fun is enjoyment! Watch the faces of your students. Are there expressions of emotion and debate, furrowed brows of concentration, knowing smiles crossing the room or just the chatter of excited groups of children creating dramas or solving the problems of the world? I HOPE SO!

They are having fun! Fun is the pure enjoyment of learning.

"Did you finish your French poster? Mine is really great."

"Meet us at recess. We want to show you our cheer."

"Let's practice our song outside."

"I can't wait to see the play."

"My mom said that if I still don't feel well I should call. I don't want to miss the presentation."

"Our history class is working on debates today. Ours is so great"

"Another assembly? We'll miss our reading time."

I love hearing these words from students as they meet each other in the hall. They are having fun in their classrooms and it shows in their attitudes, their behaviors and in the results of their efforts.

Make school fun! Motivate! Titillate! Re-create! Sublimate! Celebrate!

We want these creatures to learn about everything we've got and more!

> *"You cannot succeed by not doing things."*
> Randolph Hearst

ENTHUSIASM

The slogan for Campfire Boys and Girls is as follows:
"The first fire we light is the one within."
Our first priority is to get our kids fired up and excited about learning.

The word ENTHUSIASM comes from the Greek prefix EN meaning "within" and the word THEOS, which means "God." Put them together and you have "God within". Let's think about that for a moment. If you have God within, you are radiant...alive...passionate... powerful...living real...involved...and so on. If you aren't excited about what you are doing, how can anyone else get excited about what you are doing?

"Nothing great was ever achieved without enthusiasm."

Ralph Waldo Emerson

"Enthusiasm and success are like Siamese twins - it's hard to find one without the other."

Burke Hedges

Mel Brooks, a writer and producer of silly, off-the-wall movies speaks on why enthusiasm is crucial.

"Look, I really don't want to wax philosophic, but I will say that if you're alive, you've got to flap your arms and legs. You've got to jump around a lot. You've got to make a lot of noise, because life is the opposite of death."

ATTITUDE IS EVERYTHING

At the beginning of each school year, I join thousands of teachers in preparing classrooms with bright, colorful banners, inspirational posters, alphabets and the like.

My very favorite saying in all of this is ATTITUDE IS EVERYTHING and each year I try to find a new way to display this phrase prominently in the classroom. Having read and enjoyed the book "You Inc." written by Burke Hedges, I have found reinforcement in my belief that how you create your destiny all boils down to your attitude in life.

His friend has stated "Everyone lights up a room. Some when they enter...some when they leave." We all know the fun people, the ones who bubble over with enthusiasm and inspire us to want to change the world. It's contagious and we enjoy being around them. Then there are the "Eeyore" people who see everything as an overwhelming problem. They win the lottery and don't know what they'll do with all of that added responsibility. (Don't buy the ticket! Leave it for the rest of us who would love the responsibility.) I try to avoid these people at all costs because they too can become contagious and who needs it?

We are all players in the game of life and how we play determines our successes. What you choose to see is what you get.

What is it that you see when you look around you? Do you see a classroom filled with rude children who are demanding and difficult to handle? Then, that's what you'll get.

Do you see a room full of curious children who are diverse and interesting in their own right and who may challenge you to perform at your best? Then, you will all benefit greatly from your well-developed and well-planned lessons.

According to Burke Hedges, attitude can be defined as "a mental filter through which we process our thoughts and view the world." With the hundreds of thoughts we all have each day, we can soon comprehend how "Attitude is Everything."

CHAPTER THIRTEEN
LEARNING CHANNELS

We know that children who don't understand the concept being taught are not having fun. We also know that there are many ways in which children can learn. One of the best courses that I took on this subject was called "Teaching Through Learning Channels". It was taught by Jim McMahon and was provided to our Board in cooperation with Lesley College.

Always look into what courses are being offered by your Board . Sometimes you don't have to venture to other institutions to take valuable credit courses.

This program delved into the various ways in which we learn. We, as teachers, took the time to find out which learning style was most suitable for each of us individually. We practiced on each other and created lesson plans to suit our style. It was amazing to me how much more easily some information was learned when it was taught in the style that I could relate to best. I don't wish to bore you with too much information as I'm sure that many of you already know these channels of learning but I will list them in case you wish to refer to them at some point in the future.

ALL LEARNING IS ACCESSIBLE...WHEN YOU LEARN HOW TO ACCESS IT

There are **four types or ways in which people learn**. In other words, there are four different types of learners.

(1) The Visual Learner : The Seeing is Believing Student

(2) The Auditory Learner: The Talking, Listening Student

(3) The Kinesthetic Learner: The Action Student

(4) The Tactual Learner: The Sensitive, Feeling/Tactile, Touching Student We add to this list, two other methods of learning

(5) Olfactory learning: learning by smell: example (the wine industry) but certainly evident in a science experiment gone bad

(6) Gustatory learning: learning by taste: example (the food industry) This can be a lot of fun when studying folk arts and students cooperatively contribute food items for the class.

I am a visual learner. If I can watch something being done, I pick it up much more quickly than if someone tells me how to do it or if I have to read a set of instructions. Instructions are usually very difficult for me to follow, especially if there are no diagrams.

What an eye opener this course was to me! I felt that a door of understanding had been opened and as the weeks went on, I couldn't wait to take these lessons into my classroom. I could see light bulbs going on in children's heads and it made me wish that I had taken this course much sooner in my career. I now suggest it as a development course for every teacher to participate in. It proved to be an invaluable tool for me and my students have benefited greatly from it.

I learned that, because I was a visual learner, I often taught in that style because it was most comfortable for me. This is unfair to those students who are other types of learners. I began to teach in the other styles and found that more students were understanding the materials presented.

The most important point to glean from this is to come to the understanding that each of us learn from repetition and modeling. We teach a lesson one way, then repeat it with a twist another way.

If we can zone in on the four styles of learning and incorporate them into the regular planning process, they become an automatic part of our curriculum and a much more effective program.

Another important point to note is that **most of us use a combination of styles** to give us the best advantage for learning.

By pairing sensory activities, we can target the many ways in which children learn.

Examples: Primary/Secondary Sense

Visual/ Kinesthetic	1. Miming events in a story
	2. Creating a tableau of events in history.
	3. _____
Visual/Tactual	1. Highlighting printed words with colored markers when reading.
	2. Creating a quick time movie on the computer for presentation.
	3. _____
Visual/Auditory	1. Shooting a videotape presentation
	2. Watching a video presentation on laser disk or CD
	3. _____
Auditory/Kinesthetic	1. Reading directions while others take action
	2. Doing an "on the street" interview
	3. _____
Auditory/Tactual	1. Talking about feelings
	2. Feeling objects from a lesson placed in a bag and talking about what is felt
	3. _____
Auditory/Visual	1. Group or choral reading
	2. Teacher or student-directed visualization
	3. _____

TYPES OF LEARNING CONTINUES

Kinesthetic/Tactual
1. Taking a trust walk (blindfolded)
2. Acting out feelings in a poem
3. _____

Kinesthetic/Auditory
1. Acting out a story or poem read by others
2. Leading group in exercises or action activity
3. _____

Kinesthetic/Visual
1. Acting out lesson components
2. Collecting items outside the classroom
3. _____

Tactual/Kinesthetic
1. Students greeting other students by shaking hands or giving "high fives"
2. Acting out a peak experience in a student's life
3. _____

Tactual/Auditory
1. Describing feelings you have experienced in the past
2. Interpreting the meaning of what someone else says
3. _____

Tactual/Visual
1. Writing reflective thoughts in a journal
2. Using math manipulatives
3. _____

Add one or two more exercises to each of the senses combinations to see how you could use the pairs in your classroom. Each time you pair a primary and a secondary sense, you bring more children to the recognition and knowledge of what you are teaching. It's a fascinating practice and you can see actual results quickly.

The word "repetition" comes from its root "repeat" but it does not necessarily mean to "say" over and over. We must repeat some concepts (example -math division) in various ways in order for all of our students to accomplish success.

A very simple example: $12 \div 3 = 4$

(1) put 12 pennies into 3 even groups. This seems a bit elementary perhaps but some children will benefit from this concrete material approach. They will use it for more difficult questions and have a full understanding of how to divide

(2) $3\overline{)12}$. Use the mathematical equation and some children will get it - no problem.

(3) $3x? = 12$ Use an alternative question to show how the division works. Work backwards just to tweak the understanding of another group of children.

I know that this seems fundamental and perhaps over-simplified. I apologize if it offends anyone but, in actual fact, there are math teachers who have no problems learning math and only present the second method. They expect all of their students to "get it".

Even though each of these methods may say the same thing, they target different learning styles and, when utilized, will enable most of the learners to understand the concept of division.

Teaching a novel creatively

Let's look at teaching a novel! There are many ways to approach the novel by utilizing the learning channels,

(1) assign the reading of a chapter during Silent Reading time. (Approximately 8 out of 12 students will actually read)
(2) read each chapter aloud to the class
(3) have various prepared passages read aloud by students
(4) choose a group of students each day to read and dramatize the chapter being studied

(5) add costumes, props and setting to create a visual image while reading the chapter example: as previously mentioned - A Christmas Carol by Dickens

(6) paraphrase each chapter on the board with the class -this is a great exercise for teaching point form notes

(7) reduce the entire novel into 10 main points, teaching the plot graph and its effective way of summarizing the novel

(8) draw a pictorial representation of a chapter or create a collage of the novel's events or characters

(9) if and when there is an ethnic theme in the novel, you can prepare dishes from this culture to serve in the classroom. Often, there are many cultures represented in a class and most parents are happy to contribute both their knowledge and creative cooking for such occasions. (It's also an interesting way to introduce "curry" to children who have never experienced it before) Providing children with the knowledge of other cultures and their customs allows them to become more tolerant and accepting of the enormous and interesting diversity upon which this country is founded.

(10) create a plot graph for the novel in its entirety (use only the 10 points created in the summary)

(11) create a visual plot graph of the novel drawing its setting as a background. This method allows children to express their interpretation of the novel in art form. Some children will produce amazing results and create visuals that you had never even thought of.

(12) set up display areas for others in the school. Children create interpretive displays of the novel using various mediums. They may set up a scene for a chapter or perhaps create a few characters, costumes...anything that *your* imagination can come up with...*or theirs*.

(13) build a miniature set for the play version of the book. Include furniture and props. If you wish to have set changes, choose the set for Act One or Two or Three.

(14) create the staging for one of the acts or chapters of the book. Using diagrams and arrows, re-create the staging of the actors in the section of the book being studied. A terrific lesson is to read a play and watch it in action as the culmination of the unit. Children have the opportunity to see

how the professionals created the staging that they
themselves attempted in their project.

(15) write a book report for the novel
(16) put students into groups and assign a chapter or event per
group. This is to be presented to the class in a unique way.
Partners - Create!

Each of these assignment variations will cause another child to
pick up more information. Allow children to choose the activity that
would give them the most pleasure and accomplishment. They will
automatically express the best avenue for their learning by virtue of
their choice. Memories of events and characters will become a part of
their consciousness and students will learn more about the novel. It's
a fact!

There are many more avenues to take. Choose as many as you like
and vary your assignments as often as you can. Utilize as many
learning channels as you can to target each one of your students. They
will often help you by suggesting their own ideas so the work of
planning does not become astronomical. Often, students will do the
work of planning choices for you and all you have to do is enjoy the
creativity and evaluate accordingly. Too many times, we feel the
pressure of having to come up with "novel" ideas when, in fact,
children are one of the best resources we have at our disposal. It is a
good idea to brainstorm different ways in which to tackle any unit of
the curriculum.

"They" say - "two heads are better than one". Try thirty heads and
see what happens.

CAN YOU BECOME A MIND READER?

The following brief word list is a guide to help you listen for clues about what someone's primary learning system is. You can create your own list of words that are sensory-specific. (Taste and smell are not part of the primary system that most people use)

Keep adding to the list. It becomes fun and interesting. A game, if you will!

Visual	Auditory	Kinesthetic
see	hear	feel
look	listen	touch
image	sound	grasp
imagine	tell yourself	place yourself
brilliant	blaring	grating
sights	sounds	vibrations
light	clear	sharp
flash/lightning	thunder	clap
focus	tune in	go with the flow
shadow	echo	footprint
blind	deaf	mute

"Whenever you hear people use one set of sensory words like these you can be sure that, for the present anyway, they are thinking with or through one particular representational system. And when you use the same type of sensory language, you give them a strong sense of rapport - that you are following and understanding what they are saying. You are using the same kind of words in speech that the other person is using to think with. As though you were a mind reader!"

Mindworks

The chapter on Representational Systems in the book "Mindworks" discusses very clearly how we can communicate more effectively with others just by listening to the words they use to ask questions or describe things. It opens up a whole new "world" of understanding for both you and your students when used effectively.

CHAPTER FOURTEEN
"CHANGE — WILL DO YOU GOOD."

KEEP IT FRESH! - Some Personal Insights

I have found that I share one of the most dreaded qualities of my students. **I get bored easily.** It was quite difficult for me to accept the fact that not all of my lesson plans were as fresh and exciting as I thought they were. Each year, I would repeat some of the successful lessons from a unit I had used the year before and they would "bomb". I couldn't figure it out and often, would get very disappointed. One day, the light bulb went on

If I was repeating myself, I was probably less enthusiastic than I had originally been. Inadvertently, I took for granted the fact that the students already knew some of the material. It was not as fresh and new as the first time I had taught it, but sometimes became overdone and boring. What a horrible realization that was for me!

I learned very quickly, and to my chagrin, that students could sniff out a freshly planned unit and would respond accordingly. It was at this point that I set an important goal for myself and I wish that you would consider it also.

In order for me not to be lulled into a comfortable, possibly repetitive, boring place, I set a time limit for myself. **I would not exceed a five year maximum at any one placement.**

Although I did not always stay for the full five years, I worked very hard not to exceed the five year limit I had placed upon myself. During the course of my "teacher life", I broke my rule only once. I will go into some detail of that particular placement in order to justify my "breaking of the rule." (You may find a justification in your career as well so I wouldn't want you to feel badly.)

I taught at the phenomenal Niagara Peninsula Children's Center where I was privileged to share the lives of five year old children in a School Age Language Program. The first three years were spent teaching half-time so my total was actually 5 ½ years, two of which were spent at a satellite facility during a renovation period.

Sharing the classroom with three (totally different but each amazing) speech pathologists became one of the greatest learning experiences I have ever experienced and I will always be grateful for that rich education. (You think that having a roommate is tough. Talk to these girls about sharing a classroom with a teacher.)

In this class, some of the most creative moments of my life took place. Dramatic changes in the speech and pragmatic skills of these little ones made me feel a bit like "the Miracle Worker", even though I knew full well that I was only a member of the full team of experts guiding these children to success.

After seven years of teaching in this magical place, I knew that my time was up. You have a sense about things and you can choose to listen to your senses or you can ignore them. I chose to listen, although unwillingly, and moved on. I kept all of my admiration and respect for the team at NPCC intact and feel incredibly fortunate to have been a part of the little miracles that occurred on a daily basis. My position at this facility was a very humbling experience and I encourage anyone who has the opportunity, to work with learning or physically disabled children at some point in their career.

Many teachers tell me that they cannot teach these special children because they feel sorry for them and can't handle their "suffering". I must admit that it was difficult at the beginning but I soon came to realize that these children are just that - children. They have feelings, they have needs, they laugh and love and they, in return, need love and nurturing. They are often trapped in an uncooperative body but that does not make them any less of a CHILD. We must be able to get past our emotions of pity and learn to become the friend and teacher that they require in life. We cannot change their disability but we sure have the power to love and accept them "just the way they are" because, after all, they accept us "just the way we are" ...without condition.

"CHALLENGE"

"Why do most of us turn our heads furtively when a deformed or handicapped person comes walking down the street towards us? Is it because we feel so helpless and ill-equipped to combat the rigors of such a situation, should circumstances have been such that we had been the one chosen to walk in his footsteps?

Think about those words and as you go your way, be one of those who discover the beauty, the courage, the happiness, that can be found through these folks who walk through life sustained only by their fortitude and Faith.

All they ask of life is that which can be given through all of us who should feel it a privilege to extend it - the hand of Friendship and Love." Joanne D'Alton Clancy

HAVE THE SERENITY TO ACCEPT THINGS WITHOUT HAVING TO CHANGE THEM

It was a few years later, in a Grade 8 classroom, that I once again found myself teaching a young man who had attended the School Age Language program. His parents were unsure at that point, if they had made the right decision in bringing about his breakthrough in speech. (He had been almost non-verbal when he arrived at the Center) He hadn't stopped talking since the age of five and had reached competitive speeds when relaying information. I enjoyed every moment! He was a delightful student who did very well in school and took great pride in his accomplishments. What a wonderful gift nature had provided for me. To see the results of my work years later was a powerful lesson. I have found that these are given freely when we accept our responsibilities and act upon them. I do believe in God and his sense of humor and honor never cease to amaze me.

BE WILLING TO CHANGE

It was also a serious consideration for me to change my subject focus from time to time. Music had always been my passion and I began my teaching career in that field. Just an important note : **Just because you like a subject doesn't mean you will be great at**

teaching it. There is so much more to teaching than just liking the subject that you teach! WAKE UP CALL!!

At the beginning of my career, I had the opportunity to learn a very valuable lesson.

Having spent my first two years of full-time teaching in a home room situation, I thought I was now ready for a junior high school, teaching music on rotary to 420 students.

I had no idea how physically demanding it would be to recruit Grade 7 and 8 boys for choirs and musicals, let alone capture their interest in the every day rotary music classroom. It is a good thing that my energy levels were high because WE SANG, WE LISTENED, WE MADE INSTRUMENTS, WE PLAYED INSTRUMENTS, WE SANG, WE PERFORMED IN CHOIRS, WE PERFORMED IN MUSICALS, WE TRAVELED, WE COMPETED, WE GRUMBLED, YET WE CONTINUED TO SING.

By the age of 29, I was exhausted. My choirs had often exceeded 100 students and it was an occupation in itself to acquire, focus and maintain the attention of their members throughout the before, during and after school rehearsals. Up until this point, I had always had a weight problem. This was the one period in my life where I had the most dating possibilities and the least amount of energy to accept any of them. It was time to make a change!

My five years was up and I was moving. I interviewed for a Special Education position and was very excited when I was accepted. I found out years later that almost everyone is accepted into Special Ed. positions. The secret is how to get out of Special Education once you're in. (If you love a good challenge, there are many creative ways to do that.)

With renewed interest, I began taking courses in my "new field" of interest. That was the beginning of an amazing journey. It led me through the world of behavior problems and syndromes, physical disabilities and seizures, traumas resulting from accidents and head injuries sustained from abuse. Where the courses gave me the scientific insights, the children taught me about love, patience and courage; all of which they freely shared with me.

I remember one boy's frustration in a General Learning Disabilities class (GLD). He was so angry that he literally threw his desk out of the huge window at the side of the classroom. I couldn't begin to understand the anger and frustration that he must have been feeling to prompt such a violent outburst. It frightened me but it also gave me a new insight into the true needs of some children.

We had a piano in the classroom and often, I would just sit and play while the students worked. I had always sat down to play whenever I needed to think or just to calm myself down so I thought I'd try it . The kids would make requests and I would try to find the score for them. Not only did it enhance the music program, but it became a calming ritual during some of our more work-oriented lessons and we developed a quieter, more meaningful environment in which to work.

This angry young man seemed to relate to the music and would often just sit and enjoy the selection being played. I know that it doesn't sound like he was utilizing his time effectively but he did learn to curb much of his anger and began the process of thinking before acting out. In the world that he lived in, this was a major positive development and he was very proud of his accomplishment.

For some unknown reason, the thinking process of many people seems to improve when inspiring music is being played. Stores, offices, and manufacturing plants often play it in the background. Because not all children respond to this stimuli, try soft background music.

We would spend class time discussing our feelings and the reasons that we do what we do. I enjoyed the two years that I spent in that classroom. I remember a very supportive special education administrator, Bruce Scott, who would come in and praise us often. I don't know if he ever realized how comforting and encouraging his words were. Thank you Bruce.

Talk about Blunders

I have made some serious blunders in my years as a teacher and, although my heart was in the right place, one of my magical "brainstorms" turned out to be a total disaster.

It was nearing Christmas and I was preparing for the concert ahead. I decided that it would be a great idea to have all of the special needs children in the school learn the song "You Light up my Life". They would perform this selection to their parents and friends at the concert.

A candle was given to each member of the audience upon arrival and, at a designated time, each person was to light it. The entire student body gathered together to sing our well-practiced song. From the stage, I could hear the uncontrollable sobs of a few parents, then more and finally, the entire gymnasium of people was weeping uncontrollably. Candles were going out and soon the entire concert was an emotional disaster.

It had seemed like such a good idea at the time. Can you imagine? What was I thinking? I hear that "You Light up my Life" has been forever banned from the school and who knows what emotional scars were left behind. We all make mistakes!! I keep telling myself that but it is difficult to get over some of them. I have moved to much more upbeat music and try not to "beat myself up" too much over that incident.

It is a proven fact that the majority of teachers have "a good heart". We have to learn how and where to direct it.

Another thing we must learn is to "stick it out" when a mistake is made and try to improve it before leaving the school. Redeem yourself - eat crow - be humble and show your peers, parents and others that you will "do better next time."

Our "Space Age Christmas" the following year was much more successful as a foil covered Santa and his tiny glowing reindeer flew about the stage in a spaceship - a happy spaceship- filled with space noises and a lot of room for laughter. I was redeemed, just as you will be after your first mistake, then your second, your third...

When I had fulfilled my personal goal of duration, I accepted the hugs and well wishes, packed up my things and moved from five-year olds to a Grade 8 homeroom class where I was assigned to teach English, drama, mathematics, geography, history, art and music as well as rotary music to Grades 4-8. The next challenge awaited me and I began to create my new world again.

I can't stress this enough!

My list of Dos and Don'ts could go on and on...Here are a few

Don't become stagnant or boring.
Don't repeat yourself year after year.
Don't get stuck in a rut and be afraid to move.

Don't be afraid to take the risk of changing your subject area.
Don't worry about the "theys" of the world. You'll never meet them and if you do, it doesn't matter.

Do understand your potential to grow.
Do give yourself credit for your ability to learn and progress.
Do look at other positions that may interest you.
Do take a chance and not worry about the outcome.
Do take courses to enrich your life in order to enrich the lives of others.
Do be positive and proactive in becoming more successful than you already are.
Do look at administration as a viable way to build your leadership skills.
Do accept the fact that others are learning as well and may not have the courage to make alternative choices at the same time as you are making them.
Do look at a change as a new beginning and an opportunity for growth and new friendships.

This profession has limitless possibilities. There are so many avenues for you to take and so many enriching experiences for you to participate in that you are doing yourself a serious disservice if you don't take advantage of them.

DON'T GET STUCK IN A RUT!!

You will not benefit anyone around you, students and peers alike, and, worst of all, you will no longer enjoy this wonderful career called teaching.

"ENJOY THE PROCESS OF CHANGE, FOR IT IS ONE OF THE FEW THINGS YOU CAN RELY ON."

Don Wolfe

"CONSTANTLY BE WILLING TO EXAMINE YOUR BELIEFS ABOUT YOURSELF, OTHERS AND THE WORLD".

Winspiration

CHAPTER FIFTEEN
THE PARENT TRAP

How many times have you heard this one?

"If it wasn't for the parents, I'd have no trouble teaching these kids." or

"I don't know who I spend more time teaching - the parent or the kid." or

"If that parent would just mind their own business, everything would be fine."

Guess what? That child in your class IS THEIR BUSINESS!

Too many times teachers assume that they are in charge and that parents should "butt out."

Not True!

Parents can be your greatest asset but, if improperly treated, they can become your biggest nightmare. I'm not saying that all parents are wonderful, supportive beings who can be called upon when necessary to assist you. That's not true either.

It has been my experience that "generally speaking", parents want nothing more than for you to provide the best possible education for their child.

I can honestly say that I have met only a few parents in my lifetime who defy all normal behaviors and I have also discovered that some of these same parents have also created abnormal living conditions for their children.

Examples:

-expectations set much too high for any child to live up to

-continuous ranting and raving at their child

-frustrated single parents who are not able to cope and have to blame someone for something

-parents who insist on living their own lost dreams through their children

-parents who don't speak the language very well (and I'm not talking about foreigners here) and resort to swearing to get their point across.

Yes, we have and will continue to meet them in our travels but they are our strength builders and we can thank them for helping us to develop tact, patience and empathy for the children who have to go home to them each night.

The secret to working with all parents is to make them a part of the learning process BEFORE it begins. Inform them on a regular basis, invite their suggestions prior to starting a theme, give them time lines and valid reasons for teaching the upcoming unit on "Medieval Music" in Grade 4. (I have to each this unit because it is part of the curriculum.) Don't make excuses. Let them know that you're not particularly happy about teaching a unit that has no resources written in the language of ten and eleven year olds. (Pet peeve - sorry!)

Parents need and appreciate honesty

Be as honest with parents as you comfortably can and let them know the concerns that you may have. There is a distinct difference, however, between honesty and brutal bluntness. Learn to be tactful and try to understand their desire for their child to be "the best" that he/she can be. Allow them to share your concerns in a meaningful, supportive way. Ask for their advice in teaching their child and perhaps some of the methods that have been used successfully in other classes or even at home. Learn about some of the child's habits. Does he clean his room? Does she have pets? How does he react to...? Create generic situations where a parent can finish the sentence to present a picture of abilities and responsibilities outside of the classroom. Try to build upon the knowledge that can be provided for you quickly and readily by a parent. No one knows this child better and you can "move the information around" in order to gain a mental picture of what you may be dealing with. In many cases, children respond quite differently at home. Find out if you achieve better results or command more attention than the parent. Watch children react to their parents during visits to the school or "parent day" and see who respects and receives discipline. Don't be afraid to allow the parent to "help" you. Humility can be a good thing and this is a good place to practice it. Perhaps they know the type of learner their child is and can provide valuable input in that area. They'll be thrilled that you cared enough to ask.

Always be offensive, not defensive when it comes to handling parents.

Be proactive rather than reactive to parents. It will always hold you in good stead.

Parents have a need to be in "the Loop".

Even if there is no Loop, make one up. Parents have a need to be part of their child's "school" life because often, you see their "Rachel" more than they do.

Let's repeat that. **YOU SEE THEIR CHILD MORE THAN THEY DO.**

What if you or your partner spent 4 days in labor and gave birth to your only son or daughter who is now required to attend school all day?

To some parents; it's not fair - to others, it's a blessing and they won't bother you!

STRATEGIES FOR HAPPY PARENTS - 101

(1) At the beginning of each month: **Monthly (or so) Newsletters**
-review the units that you will be teaching in each of your subject areas
-jot down the name of the unit, the specific skills being targeted and why
-list all of the planned assignments for each unit and the time lines given. (Due dates for each section or chapter, final project dates, test dates etc.)
-decide how much class time will be given and how much homework will be expected. Compile all of this information and type it up in a letter to the parents. I sometimes attach a rubric for the major assignment to this letter. (It is a good idea to explain what a rubric is in a parent letter at the beginning of each year. Send a sample in order for them to see its purpose and value)
Leave a section at the bottom for a
Parent/Guardian signature _____

Make 2 copies of this letter for each student and send them both home. One copy is to be signed and returned to you. You then check off the name of the students who have returned them on a class list. If the signed copy is not returned within the allotted time, PHONE HOME. Make parents aware of and accountable for these notes.

The Joy of Privacy Binders

Have a privacy binder or two containing a section for class lists and one for personal pages
On the **class list pages** you can keep track of all returned items, pizza forms, etc.
On the **individual student pages**
-make anecdotal comments
-record any phone calls that you made to the home (be sure to add the date and time)
-list any allergies that the child may have
-record achievements
-record difficulties that the child may be experiencing in certain subject areas
-behavior problems should be recorded - time, date, place and with whom
-goals that the child has set and the date expected to attain them
-any awards that have been won
-extra-curricular activities that the student participates in
-a particular evening that is very busy for the child and homework should not be heavy or even assigned (this one is very important as it can cause the child a great deal of unnecessary stress if work can't be modified or made up in class)

My binder contains a page designated for each student in the class. It is my confidential working copy. I do not share it!!!!

A privacy binder is just that - private! It is to be used for your own information and resource. It should contain strategies that you have tried for the difficulties that your students exhibit and are still working on. Whenever a parent interview comes up, it can be used as a very accurate reference book.

By following the "monthly news" procedure, you have eliminated the dreaded 8:45 a.m. calls to the school.
Example:

"I had no idea that Theodore had an assignment due today. He never tells me anything."

"If I had known that a major assignment was due, I would have helped her to complete it."

"How can we help our daughter with her homework if we don't know what's going on?"

Believe it or not, a parent who knows that they cannot complain about missing projects, won't!

You have put the ball in their court and have made them accountable.

I keep all of the letters being sent home in a separate binder labeled **"Monthly News"**. It becomes your greatest back-up file and you can photocopy any letters again for that child whose starving pet mistook it for a treat and wolfed it down on the way home. It's also handy to have as a referral when you can't remember exactly what the time line was for a certain assignment. It keeps you on track just as much as the children.

(2) Pick up the Phone

As soon as you notice that a child is falling behind (2 or more assignments), CALL HOME!

Don't complain to the parent but **ask for their advice** on how to motivate their child to complete assigned work. Let them accept some of the responsibility for their child's school work. If their suggestion doesn't work, they tend not to blame you because, after all, it was their idea.

Record each and every phone call that you make on the child's information page in "THE BINDER". You could even write a brief point form synopsis of the conversation. If it's a real "sticky" one, have your principal sign your summary to keep him/her on board. When parents know you have nothing to hide, they tend to have more respect and don't wield as much power against you.

(3) Invite Parents In

Whenever you are scheduling a special art class or a presentation of projects, invite a parent or two to come in and help or observe. I have sometimes invited a parent from another class in to help with a particularly difficult art lesson. They tend to help all of the children rather than just their own and they are thrilled for the compliment of being asked. It's a good practice to become acquainted with "other" parents in the school, even if you are not teaching their child that year. It makes for good relationships all around. There are so many talented parents out there and many of them would love to come in and help you "on occasion", not on a regular basis because that involves a commitment. (And you may not wish to have that one back again - oops!)

To avoid stress, deal with one thing at a time, one parent at a time, one activity at a time; whatever feels comfortable for you because **REMEMBER -YOU ARE IN CHARGE.**

(4) **Train parents carefully**

A very important trap to avoid is that parent conference in the hallway at 8:30 in the morning just as you are heading out for yard duty or grabbing that last cup of coffee to "steel you" for the morning. That is your time and you should choose what you wish to do with it. There is nothing worse than a chatty parent who nails you at the exit door on your way out to the only lunch date you can fit into your weekly schedule.

Explain very politely in your FIRST newsletter of the year, that you will be "happy" to meet with any parent during a scheduled meeting. They may call the office at any time and you will return their call as soon as possible to set up a mutually beneficial time for both of you.

BE FIRM! Do not allow them to corner you in the hallway for even a casual discussion about their child's behavior, academic achievement or sports events. Keep rerouting them to the office and they will eventually get the message. Use tactful phrases like:

"I would love to meet with you. Please make an appointment with our secretary."

"I am very busy right now but if you would go to the office and make an appointment, I'll get back to you."

"I would like to have all of the information at my fingertips, so I'll call you to set up an appointment."

No rudeness here; just a firm NO will suffice. **You will not lose the respect of a parent**. In fact, you may gain some for "sticking to your guns."

MY FAUX-PAS

I wish to stress this over and over because I fell into a very bad trap and was caught like a deer in the headlights of a car. Please learn from my mistake as I share my experience with you.

We were preparing a school yearbook on a fairly sophisticated computer program. The program was being taught in-depth to all of the Grade 8 students and each person was designated a responsibility for its completion. During one of the regular library classes, an unknown student, obviously very skilled on the computer, ventured into our restricted program and began rearranging the heads on some of the photographs. We had no idea who it was but it was very disconcerting to the students in charge of that section of the book.

After careful, non-accusatory questioning of a few children in the library class, it was resolved that a few boys had played with the pictures and "could have been" responsible for this act of "silliness." The three boys in question admitted to having "played with pictures" but didn't feel that any harm was done. Their library privileges were revoked for a period of two weeks.

The following day, after school, I met the mom of one of the boys in the hallway and mentioned that there had been some foul play with the computer yearbook program and that her son had admitted to playing with the pictures. I explained that he and two other boys were being punished for breaking the rules of conduct in the library. Their computer privileges were being revoked for a period of two weeks. As a class, we had chosen this as a fair and equal punishment and had left it at that. I asked that she discuss it with him as I did not wish the yearbook to be sabotaged any further. At the time, I was confident that I had shared my feelings in a truthful, friendly, even light-hearted manner.

This mother took my information home and it became a HUGE and GROSSLY misinterpreted conversation. It had been blown severely out of proportion and taken very defensively when it was merely meant to comment on the rules of the computer lab and why her son had been suspended from it for two weeks. At the time, no one had accused her son of sabotaging the "entire" yearbook.

The next evening, she and her husband insisted upon a meeting with both the principal and I to resolve this issue. I'm sure that they expected an apology or "something"(possibly my resignation). I worked very hard to clarify my intentions but to no avail. It became a very emotional "she said, she said" and nothing was resolved. To this day, the mother goes out of her way to avoid me.

Had I had the presence of mind to ask for an interview with both parents and, in the company of my principal, to discuss the rules and code of conduct while using the computers in the lab, I would have saved myself a lot of grief.

Appointments are a necessity. You are not being rude. You are covering yourself and making sure to conduct as accurate a meeting as possible. Inviting a principal or resource teacher into a "dicey" meeting is definitely suggested. You want to be sure that the information you share is given in a non-threatening, clear and positive way. If a child is causing a problem, try to have suggestions for improvement ready to share. Parents are emotional and we have to be considerate of those emotions. The hallways are not the place to have any serious student discussions. Take it from this sometimes over-friendly "impulse queen."

(5) **Choose parent volunteers wisely**

Let's face it! There are parents out there who love to supervise class trips because they have a true desire to support the staff in providing a safe, memorable and fun experience for the children, the main focus of all of our trips.

Then you have the parent who systematically collects every detail of their interpretation of what went on in order to provide full coverage to the entire community on their return. These are the journalistic "wanna-bes" whose life is not yet fulfilled and somehow require some sort of recognition. Facts seem vaguely familiar to those who were part of the trip, but somehow seem a little "off".

According to one particularly intuitive reporter, "one of the teachers could have slept with someone - maybe", a student almost fell to his death while hanging hundreds of feet in the air from the top balcony, the teachers all went drinking after "lights out" and she couldn't find any staff in the hotel at four in the morning.

What this messenger failed to relate to inquiring minds was that the highest floor that our students were housed on was the third. Two security guards were stationed at opposite sides of both the boys' and the girls' separate floors and, the once energetic staff who had kept up with 65 teenagers all day long, had fallen into bed when the security guards arrived. Believe me, no staff member wishing to be involved in a "one night stand", would consider such a momentous decision on a school trip surrounded by huge numbers of curious eyes and ears.

If you want to have an affair, the first step is...oh, sorry... another book.

No teaching soul would be found anywhere but in bed at 4:00 a.m., recouping for the next day's events. My question? "Why was this mother roaming the halls of the Holiday Inn at 4 a.m.?"

Be Aware - Be very Aware

You will be informed of and become quite adept at recognizing the "thrill-seekers". Avoid them at all costs! Have a list of staff names ready when "they" apply for the job of volunteer. The key is to always smile politely and once again thank them for offering when you and your trustworthy handpicked volunteers have sworn an "oath of silence" and arrived safely back at the school with all children intact.

It's not that anything "bad" happens on these trips but some little things that children do can be blown out of proportion by some parent volunteers. I don't like the fact that a child is judged by an inappropriate action on a trip. Sometimes children have never experienced being "out there" and there should be room for understanding and acceptance of new exposures. There have been times where **my** tolerance levels are not where they should be and **I know these children well**. A parent coming on the trip, who does not have the background knowledge or the patience to deal with a "unique" individual, could change the entire experience of the outing in the eyes of the community.

If children do something drastically wrong, they are usually dealt with at the time or the parents are notified to come and pick them up. In all of my years of teaching, we have never had such a difficult problem that it couldn't be handled on the trip by the staff in charge. Good parent volunteers understand that many children are in the learning process even more so on a trip and respect that fact. Over the years, I have had my "favourites" and will always remember the time and dedication given by them, enabling us to provide safe, happy,

149

fun-filled experiences for curious, maturing children. They know who they are! Thank you!!!!!!

(6) **Stick to your guns**

When you have to make a decision regarding your class, program, club, sports team or choir, it is your decision to make. Make the decision fairly, give valid reasons for your decision and STAND FIRM!

Be sure to have your principal on board. Most principals will appreciate and understand your decision and support your endeavors. (After all, much of the preparation for these groups does not take place during school hours and they appreciate your "extra" hard work and effort)

I have taught choirs during most of my teaching years. It is my passion and I derive a great deal of pleasure from it. As I have mentioned, some of my choirs reach 100 or more in number and I sometimes have to make awkward or difficult decisions when we are asked to perform.

It is often my habit to teach one part (soprano or alto) to one class and the other part to another class. During this particular Christmas season, I had taught the soprano part of the program of songs to 2 different classes and the alto part to the 2 remaining classes. The choir involved over 100 children in the junior division. Because we were so amazing, we were often asked to perform at various functions or in special places. (I say this because I truly believe it). This particular request came from a company who could only provide space for approximately 50 students to perform. Here comes the problem!

Making choices is difficult and I always try to make them **as fair and impersonal** as possible.

My home room class would definitely be performing because their teacher would be absent, so that was elementary. They had been taught the soprano part so there was the top group. I now needed altos who were strong enough to offset my class of amazing vocalists. My Grade 6 class did a beautiful job. The Grade 4s had learned alto as well but they were young and not as strong so I chose the more mature singers. The Grade 4 class and the split 5/6 class (my other soprano group) would be left behind. I knew at the outset that 2 of the junior classes would not be able to perform AT THIS PARTICULAR

TIME so I made the most logical choice that I could. I had avoided choosing special children, blocking out behavior problems, etc.

In my mind, this decision was cut and dried. It was fair and I explained it carefully to the entire choir who seemed to understand and agree. They knew that they were practicing for much larger concerts during the next two weeks and all of them would be performing. They also agreed that this concert would provide positive exposure for our school and would assist in our fund-raising efforts. The principal saw the logic in this decision, agreed with it and the notes went home to parents.

Would you think that this would create a huge problem? Neither did I.

During the next two days I could see a **handful** of parents individually rushing past my classroom to the office and complaining about my tactics." How could I be so unfair to the other two classes?" was the big question.

These few banded together and openly threatened to take their children to the performance themselves if I didn't put them on the bus. Did ONE SINGLE PARENT approach me? Not a chance. That would have been too logical and I might have made sense. They badgered our unfortunate principal who, thankfully, stuck to his guns and said "No" to their demands.

An hour before the bus arrived, a couple of those tenacious parents loitered around the door of their child's classroom during lunch. I stuck my head in the opposite door and firmly reminded the teacher (who was very supportive) that NO CHILD FROM HIS CLASS WOULD BE PERFORMING EVEN IF THEY ARRIVED AT THE CONCERT. If they came with their parents, they would be welcome as part of the audience but I would only be conducting a choir of fifty children.

I think that my voice must have carried as planned because there were no "surprise" guests. Did I make friends and influence people? Perhaps not; BUT, they'll know to trust and be sure that I will keep my word in future.

I am not angry with those parents for the way they felt. I came to the realization later on, that they had actually demonstrated an understanding of one of my goals. Approaching me with demands and having no viable solution is an effort in futility because I had created that rule for myself and, quite obviously, for them.

My decisions stand firm UNLESS there is a better way. I have, from time to time, listened to valid parental concerns and modified my plans, but never at the expense of being unfair to any children.

Had that tiny handful of parents been able to provide a better alternative, I would have listened. I AM ALWAYS WILLING TO LISTEN. Obviously, there was no better way, so this group of four approached "my superior" in an attempt to wield their power.

A wise leader once told me that a great principal is not your superior but your support. I have learned this to be true at different times in my career and have the greatest respect for those who have lived up to that statement. They have made me want to be a better teacher.

I have set out the following rules that I use when confronted with some serious decision-making.

Do your best to make good choices.

Get your principal on board.

Explain the reasons for making the choice that you did.

Send notes home to parents with the explanation.

Be willing to listen if there are acceptable alternatives.

Decide which decision is the best for both the children and your program.

When all is said and done - STAND FIRM!

Never be afraid to stand firm when you have legitimate reasons for what you are doing. Again, I reiterate; it is **your** job, **your** role, **your** responsibility...and you have to make it fit YOU!

PARENTS CAN BE A GREAT RESOURCE

The strategies that I have been discussing have been successful tools in building relationships and respect with the parents of the children that I have taught. As I have stated, parents have a need to be informed and included in the education process. This is not an unfair request, nor should it be an uncomfortable one. You should never fear a parent. You are the professional who is making a lifetime career of teaching children. If they have a problem with you, take an honest look at yourself to see if you could be doing something differently to help them. Stay consistent and strong, positive and supportive and if they can't see eye to eye with you, at least allow them to respect you for your goals and values.

You are the expert. Take courses which provide answers for uncertain areas, keep resources and booklets on different topics handy and make these informational materials available to interested parents. Whenever there is a good course available for parents, invite them along or provide the information for them to attend. It may surprise you when a mother or father takes up your offer to attend a parenting seminar or a workshop that deals with ADHD. If you can attend with them, you have bonded. That parent will work with you all year and help you to achieve your goals in teaching their child successfully. Never underestimate the power of a teacher-parent relationship. When it's good - it's very good.

IN SUMMARY

Whenever I have any spare time, I peruse parenting magazines for interesting and informative articles that I can cut out and add to my repertoire of resources. I ask the parents of my students to do the same and receive a lot of positive feedback and many good articles.

I have been blessed with the opportunity of meeting many fine "parents" in this career. I have acquired new friends whose children I have taught and watched marry. I have attended baptisms and baditzvahs and have even taught the offspring of students from my early years. (Yikes!)

In general, parents are wonderful and supportive. They can make your day, your week and your year. Throughout my career, their cards, gifts and well wishes have carried me through many difficult times. My filing cabinet is filled with mementos that I read on "blue days". They are my strength and my acquired wealth.

Don't ever underestimate the positive power of supportive parents. Their smiles of encouragement are worth more than your paycheck when you need a lift. Be grateful for them, build bridges with them and work with them to build the future of our teaching profession for, if treated well, they will become your greatest advocates.

"AUTHORITY"

"Tread softly if you are one who is granted a semblance of power during this lifetime, for power can become a heady, intoxicating wine with one's usual reactions becoming distorted and excessive. Do not abuse this sacred trust. A careless mistake, a wrong interpretation, can be the trigger-finger of a chain of events which could lead to disaster for the individual concerned.

Many leaders of the world often become so self-engrossed in their own ability to crack the whip, as it were, that power in their hands becomes a tool of self-destruction, as well as the destruction of those whose lives they may touch, directly or indirectly.

Power and moral responsibility go hand in hand."

Joanne D'Alton Clancy

CHAPTER SIXTEEN
HOMEWORK

This chapter follows the Parent Chapter on purpose because I feel strongly that parents have a lot to do with "Homework completion." (Not necessarily at the age of sixteen because I can't get my son to take a book out of his backpack, let alone carry it to a desk and read it)

I would like to broach this subject with great caution as it seems to be as personal an issue as buying lingerie. (Sorry guys!)

What I will do is share some of my experiences with you. Ultimately, you have to make it work for you. I wish to address mainly the elementary teachers in this section because secondary education has different requirements at different levels and I don't pretend to know what's best for those teachers who plan their subject areas so carefully.

The following points deal with the various aspects of homework. They do not reflect anyone else's opinions but my own and those with whom I have dealt. There are some valuable insights, however, and I urge you to read them carefully. Obviously, at the end of this chapter, you will still be in charge of your own limits and expectations. Hopefully, this will provide some general knowledge for you to consider.

(1) **Homework is...**

A) **assigned as the completion of the expected day's work.**

As you know, not all children work at the same pace. If primary children have been given seat work and it was not completed in class, that would be a worthwhile, beneficial homework assignment. It puts all of the children on the same page for the next day.

If every child in the class (or almost every child) has incomplete work at the end of the day, you may have set work levels and expectations that were too high. Once in a while, it happens and that is to be expected, but if it becomes routine - pull back!

Remember this - If your average and above average students have work to complete each day, where does that put the children who are struggling? They are already slower to complete the task. Now, they get to take it home and struggle twice or three times as long as many of their peers. Are they having fun? Do you think that will continue to enjoy your class? Do you think that classroom work will improve?

I have observed this situation during my evaluation visits to various schools and have found that some students will no longer make the effort to be neat, accurate or even eager to please. They will finish that work at all costs.

It won't matter what the results are because "it is finished and I don't have to do boring homework."

ADAPT! ADAPT! ADAPT!

It is also important to note that not all children have to complete 20 questions to understand the concept. Children who work more laboriously could benefit from completing 15 questions or 10 accurately rather than the full 20 rushed through quickly, inaccurately and even without real thought.

There is no rule that states "All children must complete all questions." They should understand what is being taught. Gauge carefully!

I have met some intermediate students who couldn't have cared less about the outcome or grade. At first I didn't realize that they were swamped with too much work. Once the light bulb went on, I tried to adapt to their limits. As the work load decreased and an end was in sight, their pride levels changed. They knew that they could actually complete the assignment and then went on to try for accuracy. Some of these children achieved excellent results but in fewer questions.

Never give a child reason to feel that they don't care, because often it is because they just can't handle the workload.

If this is happening you may hear, "It's done and that's what you wanted, isn't it?"

It's sad to think that a teacher's insistence upon completing the full assignment could have priority over the actual understanding of the concept or lesson.

B) assigned at the end of the day as a task to be completed for the next day?

I SURELY HOPE NOT!

I have met and worked with teachers who delight in handing out a nightly homework assignment at 3:00 p.m. as a part of their daily routine. The funny thing is that they actually expect all of their students to complete it for the next day.

I'm sorry but this infuriates me!!!!!!

I have three children of my own. During their elementary school life, they delighted in participating in various sports programs, skating, dancing, visiting grandparents and cousins, shopping (my personal favorite) and other fun, social, character-building activities. I gave birth to these curious creatures and I wanted some quality time with them too.

It broke my heart when I returned to full-time teaching. After the birth of my daughter, I had enjoyed 10 years of part-time teaching and continuing my education. During that time, I produced two more offspring and had built my schedule around my youngsters' nap times and appointments; shared their lunchtime and school trips, and actively enjoyed their presentations and speeches during school hours. I missed them terribly and couldn't wait to get home to share some "fun" things until their bedtime, after which I would tackle my own homework. Returning to a full day schedule meant that I had to rely on the evenings to provide this sharing time.

My children had dance lessons and sports events during the week nights and we visited libraries on a regular basis to find good books for bedtime. Weekends were the perfect time for flea markets, garage sales, shopping in open-air markets (we seldom missed a Saturday), clothes and accessory shopping at any mall within a sixty mile radius and traveling to visit relatives and out-of-town friends. I wanted to take full responsibility for the "other" education that my children required.

There is a lot more to children than their academic standing and, even though schools provide a great deal of activities, children need to "PLAY" with neighbors, cousins, friends and siblings.

I resented the teachers who tried to take the time for these experiences away from me by assigning hours of after school work. From them, I learned many valuable insights regarding my own teaching philosophy.

TEACHERS ARE NOT RESPONSIBLE FOR FILLING THE EVENINGS OF THEIR STUDENTS AND WE CERTAINLY DO NOT HAVE THE RIGHT TO TAKE AWAY THEIR CHILDHOOD.

I actually had a mother approach me after school one day late in October and demand that I give her son more homework because he was bored in the evenings and was watching too much television. I can almost remember verbatim what my answer was because I was astounded at her request.

"Mrs._____ I did not give birth to your son. I am his teacher and I do fulfill that role during the time he is in my care. If you would like him to have more homework, then I suggest you give it to him."

I can't believe that there are parents (and I know they exist) who feel happiest when their child is sitting at a desk completing another three hours of schoolwork every evening. They actually brag about it to their friends!

I have never supported the notion that there should be a two hour minimum of assigned homework each evening and I definitely don't believe that weekends are a regular time for homework assignments (because the child has more time?).

Children need to become well-rounded individuals . While I agree that school provides much of the foundation for this, I feel that the extra-curricular activities that I have mentioned earlier provide meaningful and very necessary experiences.

I do encourage every child to read each night for at least ½ hour if possible but I don't put this into the homework category. It can provide enjoyment when it becomes part of a routine. There are many worlds to explore in fascinating books and I do ask parents to support me in my quest for building more avid readers.

As an adult, I chose a profession which does require me to complete a lot of extra homework and I do it when everyone has settled in for the night. Children, on the other hand, are the ones who need to settle down after a long day of work and play. It doesn't mean "quiet time", it means "different time". I believe in the old adage "a change is a rest". Children need a change from the full day of schooling and play. They need a change of pace, scenery and activities.

Completing assigned class work or working on projects on occasion is totally acceptable, even required, but having to add another three hours of work on to a school day borders on "kidnapping childhood".

C) completing one major assignment per unit or theme.

The other part of this is that **I do not assign any major assignment or project exclusively as homework.** I generally have the children research, complete point form notes, and do much of the compilation of their project in class. I like to supervise the various stages of a project, especially in the elementary grades in order for them to create good habits. If they are doing the work at home, mistakes can be made and worked on for hours, things often need to be undone, and I have found that many parents pass my Grade 8 geography course by virtue of their perfect projects.

We are teachers. We teach, supervise, correct mistakes, set examples and visually instruct our expectations and correct procedures in completing the work we have assigned. I like to watch the progress of "my kids". I like to see where they break down and what sort of help they need. Often, parents cannot help their child because they do not have the background knowledge required for that particular subject matter. The end results are much more accurate and successful if the project has been dealt with under your watchful eye. There is less frustration, an obvious pride in their own work and a **significantly more accurate evaluation can take place**.

D) another issue including "Groups".

If you pair two, three or even four children up for a project LOOK AT THE GEOGRAPHIC LOCATIONS OF THEIR HOMES and the after school activities of each child in the group. Parents have nightmares when trying to get a group of children together to work on a project. It is unfair of us to expect a handful of children who do not drive, who may live great distances apart and who have totally different interests and clubs after school, to try and go through the frustration and stress of completing a group project after school.

My children have generally attended small, country schools. Often, the nearest child in the class lived at least two miles away. Whenever my daughter had to complete a project after school, we parents would have to arrange rides, meals, car pooling children to another activity following the session... you catch my drift. Being a parent and a teacher is a great way to find out how legitimate your

159

demands really are. If you are not a parent, interview a conscientious mother of two or three children and set up a questionnaire with pertinent questions. Sounds silly? It will really help you. Never underestimate the power of a good questionnaire or survey.

"Make a sincere effort to put yourself into the place of your students' parents before you assign after school projects and activities."

HOMEWORK - MAKE IT COUNT

Homework is...
E) **setting realistic expectations.**

I have had conversations with quite a few teachers who get very annoyed that their students do not visit the public library to research the assigned project. As I listen more closely, I learn that the students were instructed on Tuesday to have the research information by Friday. The children had three nights to visit the library and they did not.

Let's look at the possible explanations.

(1) Parents work shift work and cannot drive their child to the library during that particular week

(2) Children don't live anywhere near the public library and have no transportation to get there

(3) Researching a project requires quite a bit of time and some parents are unavailable for that length of time on the nights in question

(4) It often requires money to print and photocopy information from the computer or reference books (they cannot leave the library) and the parent may not have a pay day until next week

(5) If, living on a farm, the child has many other responsibilities to complete before he/she can even consider leaving the house

(6) In this day and age, many people are caring for elderly parents in their own home. They do not feel comfortable leaving them alone while taking their child on an unplanned trip to the library. Schedules are often created weeks at a time to arrange various outings.

Don't burden your students with unexpected expectations. Give advance notice in your newsletter and allow the parents the luxury of planning and coordinating special activities and trips on their calendar. Suggest library times and research models as part of your time line when sending project expectations home in the form of a letter.

My daughter is in her last year of elementary school as I write. I am very busy with many new projects in my life and I use my daily planner to organize everything. Her activities and appointments take precedence over my plans and I try very hard to work around her schedule.

I need some warning and appreciate a newsletter that informs me in advance of upcoming events. (Track and field, school talent shows, theater trips, school trips) I plan my life around these things and then I fill in the blanks. We make the effort to check her backpack when she arrives home in order to catch all of the notices that sometimes get "lost" in the crunch of morning schedules. An unexpected demand with no notice is often an impossible task for me to help her with and we scramble to accommodate her as best we can. Often, it just cannot be accomplished. I also have a son... My other daughter sometimes needs... It's great when there are two parents to pull from but in many cases, that's not a reality.

HOMEWORK SHOULD BE A CONSTRUCTIVE THING

Homework is...

F) **becoming aware of your students' "after school life".** This is part of your homework assignment. I have been invited to attend many hockey games, song and dance recitals, Christmas plays, tournaments and other activities by my students and their parents. I try to get to as many as possible because it makes me more aware of their "after school life". It gives me more understanding, even tolerance, the morning after. I generally bring my own children along and find these events to be wonderful outings. My daughter began to look forward to the opportunity of watching live hockey. (I have not nor have I ever been a great fan of a game where grown men smash each other into boards to acquire a small, black piece of rubber which they can't hang on to for more than a millisecond) She has developed a sincere admiration for the game. I have even "sort of" enjoyed a few games myself. My cheering skills have improved and I can relate better to "hockey moms".

My students have become acquainted with my family, I became a little more involved with theirs, and many mutual benefits have evolved from these experiences. I could always discuss general issues like homework or a current assignment with a parent who could clarify concerns and provide important feedback in a non-threatening environment.

It never became a personal interview and their comments were a very important part of my planning. Parents have always been a part of my support group in making decisions and plans. I ask for advice and often take it. Many times, I tailored my projects and longer assignments around the demanding schedules of my students and it promised better results every time.

If you are a new teacher to the school, make your expectations known at the outset. Create a parent survey and ask relevant questions like:

1) Which after school activities does your child participate in?
2) How often does your child participate in after school activities?
3) How much homework do you feel that your child can handle each evening?
4) Would you prefer not to have homework assigned on the weekend?

Please give reasons to support your answer.

Add as many questions as you like. Make it as in-depth or as detailed as you wish. You are the author and you have needs to fulfill.

You can make this a check list or a more involved written survey. It's going to the parents, not the children, so you can expect accurate and honest answers. Cater your program to the needs of that class and change those needs each year as the majority of parent desires warrants it. Be sure to hand these out early in the year. Read them carefully! Respond to the letters with a plan of attack for the first term. You may follow the same pattern each term or change it accordingly. Explain the results of your survey to all parents in the newsletter. BE PROACTIVE!!

I guarantee that if you have the **majority of parents** on your side, your classroom will become a happier, more successful place and you will be a happier, more fulfilled teacher. Share the load with your allies - **"they'll have a lot more respect for you in June."**

IN SUMMARY

- suit the expectations of your homework to the child (in number, degree of difficulty, etc.)
- do not make homework an overwhelming part of their day
- homework should support learning, not be a separate subject
- give parents the option of providing positive character-building experiences after school
- trust parents to educate their own children after school in the many character-building activities that they have chosen
- don't put added stress on yourself each day by having to routinely mark extra work
- provide the option of "extra" assignments for the children who request or would benefit from more practice "on occasion" (I had a student who would constantly come and ask for extra math sheets because he enjoyed doing them - go for it!)
- have homework sheets available in class for those who complete work early or want more work
- encourage at least ½ hour of time to be set aside for reading. If you wish, make it a homework assignment. It is realistic and will prove to be beneficial for the child in many ways, one of which is a calming and relaxing way to retire.
- do become aware of your students' "after school life" and, whenever possible, JOIN IN!

CHAPTER SEVENTEEN
HE/SHE HAD TO BE SOMEBODY'S BABY

I can promise you that you will meet at least one child in your travels who will give you certain grief. He or she will become your nemesis and you will spend nights awake wondering how to deal with "this one."

There are so many reasons for children to be the way they are and we can look for all sorts of excuses for their behavior. The fact is, that no matter what the reason, they are a pain in the b_. It would be wonderful if we could find out what the underlying difficulty is and sometimes, we actually get lucky. (I'll share a story with you on that subject a little later on in this chapter.)

Sometimes, kids are just "spoiled rotten", expecting everything and anything they ask for. It can be as simple as that. These are the ones that I find the most difficult to deal with. There isn't much you can give them that they don't already have so you set up your rules and boundaries and give them the discipline that may be lacking.

There have been students who have tried to "break me" by giving me their best shot when it came to causing headaches. You know the kind. They knot in your forehead and then slowly gather strength as they attack the entire skull. I have learned that "I don't back down. I hold most of the cards and I tend to accept a good challenge."

You are the boss and what you say goes. If they don't like it, that's what the door is for. It leads to another place, a quiet place, where they can't disturb others or talk back to you on a regular basis.

Most of these children require an audience and when there is none, they get "bummed". With your principal and resource teacher, find a suitable spot in the school where this child can have a "quiet time", a supervised place where only he/she can work. With no audience and no one to yell at except an indifferent party, this place can become their regular classroom if they wish.

We had a nurse's room in one of the schools where I taught. On occasion, it had a nurse in it, but I don't think that you have to worry about that any more, what with all of the cutbacks.

The room was joined to the office and it became the "quiet place" for a certain student. He spent quite a few hours in there at the beginning and soon found that it got lonely. He was only excused for an occasional supervised washroom break and possibly recess depending on how much had been accomplished. The classroom teacher would visit at regular intervals to check his progress and sometimes allowed him to return until his behaviors led him back.

The visits to the classroom became more numerous and he began to adapt to the classroom rules and routines. He was never an exemplary student but he learned "who the boss was" and managed to deal with it most of the time. This is just one of the many strategies that you and your staff can come up with to deal with behavioral problems and I was fortunate to always have a very supportive resource teacher available.

That's not what this chapter deals with, however. We can find a lot of "get them out of my hair" strategies and "live" through the experience of having that student in our class, but how do we touch them? How do we make a difference? How do we become teachers who will encourage and take on the task of dealing with them rather than sending them away?

VERY IMPORTANT ASPECT OF CHILDREN

I learned an amazing lesson when I gave birth to my oldest daughter. I LOVED THIS BABY WITH ALL OF MY HEART AND I LOVED THE OTHER BABIES IN THE NURSERY TOO. It struck me how powerful that realization was. I would have done anything to protect those tiny little creatures who had just entered this world in their vulnerable and fragile state. If I could take this feeling into my classroom and relate it to every child there, I might be on to something.

Tough kids gave me headaches but this was a new angle for me. I would try to see them as the special gift that they were to their own mother. I just got them a little later but I still had to teach and protect them.

I began to envision my students as babies, I had them bring in their baby pictures for my "Wall of Interest" and I took a serious look at how to deal with them in a more loving and forgiving way. Their black leather jackets were merely "black Winnie the Pooh baby

165

outfits" and I would become amused rather than angry. I smiled more, I reasoned more and I tried harder to find out what circumstances had brought them to become the "prickly personality" they were. This was the beginning of a new chapter in my "Teacher Life".

A few months after returning to teaching (our maternity leaves were 16 weeks long and I returned half-time because I couldn't stand to be away from my child any longer than four hours at a time), I met a young man who hated school. I was the Principal's relief, a fancy title for "you teach everything that the busy principal doesn't have time for". It changed from year to year and so could my position and school placement at any time if there were cut backs. My assignment was to teach English to two classes, art to one class, and math to one class. No wonder the principal couldn't handle the work load. Either that or they just gave me what was left and called it Principal's Relief instead of Smorgasbord teacher.

This young man landed in my English class (which did give me something to work with because art was my other subject and stick people were my specialty in that department). He hated to read, he couldn't print or write and his vocabulary was much more appropriate for the local factory which produced automobiles. (no offense, but I've encountered that whole "factory" world of speech) Various comments on report cards in his student file all told me that he had a bad attitude, didn't try and was a very low student.

I read all of his data carefully but, in my mind, I added that he was cute, though. He had a great smile when it snuck out and he wouldn't flinch when I touched his shoulder in a punchy motion in the hall. I had something to work with here. He didn't seem to hate me yet and I began my mission.

He had to be somebody's baby. He must have had a thick mop of black hair and saucer-like chocolate eyes. A small cleft in his chin was a definite facial boost and his dimples were deep. I tried to envision the happiness that his fortunate mother would have felt as the nurse handed her this little dumpling and I began to feel the emotions of my own "new motherhood day."

We started to have casual conversations when there was no one around, often after school when I asked him to stay. He began to help me clean the blackboards, carry things to the office and car and look forward to checking out my latest package of baby pictures. (Being a new mother, I carried a new batch of developed photos in my purse at all times. Later on, I was given a "brag book" to keep special ones in) He really liked cars a lot and was hoping to one day become a mechanic. That was a breakthrough for me because I happened to know a "guy" who had a car dealership and loved to putter with an old '35 Ford he had been building for years. I decided to hook them up one weekend and the rest is history.

The two of them got along famously. This boy had no father and this "guy" had no kids. They had a lot of similar interests in building the car and they began to see each other on a more regular basis. (Which I had nothing to do with)

I believe that it was because I had taken the time to find out something of interest for this student that he began to show an interest in my classes. He read the car magazines that I dug up at garage sales and flea markets and he would rewrite many articles in his own words to explain them to me. Eventually, his written work became clear enough for me to understand without having to ask him what everything meant.

He asked questions and started a "word list" book. The dictionary was difficult for him to follow so we bought a junior dictionary and didn't share that information with anyone. It was covered by a creative "collage" book jacket and the kids thought he carried a special car book around. By the end of the year, (about seven months at our school) I could see the sparkle in his eyes as he attempted new things and the feeling of pride he exhibited when they were completed correctly. He was still behind academically, but he was making great strides and I knew he could go on to a technical institute or study car mechanics. He was motivated and seemed more content with himself.

Did I perform a miracle? Hardly.

Did I take an interest in a boy who seemed angry and unfulfilled? Yes.

Had I used my previous attitude, I would have sent him to the resource room most of the time and missed out on a wonderful relationship. I never did find out the reason that he was so angry, we never did get that far, but I know that his anger began to dissipate ever so slowly because I was privy to one of those "twists of fate" occurring a few years later.

I Love Twists of Fate

I was invited to the wedding of one of my past co-op students. She had been with me for two different placements over a two year period and we had become friends. Her mom was a great baker and would send in samples and recipes for us to try with the children in the class. (Her sugar cookies were the best!)

This girl had a boyfriend who came to pick her up each day and would often come in for a chat. A few years later, my husband and I received an invitation to their wedding and I was delighted. Upon arriving at the reception, I was greeted by none other than "my special friend". I was shocked to see him again because it had been quite a few years since we parted. My daughter was now well into her teenage years and he had moved away shortly after graduating from Grade 8. He had grown into a very handsome young man who looked very content and happy.

My first question, of course, was "So, what are you doing now?"

He gave me that incredible, dimpled smile and replied, "I sell cars, Mrs. Hearn. My partner and I own a small Mercedes Dealership in _____ and I handle the parts and service department as well. I'd like you to meet my girlfriend."

At this point, he turned to her and said, "This is the teacher I told you about."

If you can use my philosophy, please do, because it can provide a new attitude and a new way of looking at your behavior problem students. We can't always figure out what makes them tick but something does. I have had students that I could never reach and they caused me heartache and grief but I had to resign myself to the fact that had I tried my best and they did not respond. Perhaps one day, they will take pause and think of the methods I used to try and reach them.

One of "those boys" is presently in the Kingston Penitentiary and I can't begin to feel the pain his parents must deal with.

PERSPECTIVE

"Each individual regards the same situation in a different light. Depending upon our environment, our upbringing, and our heritage, we see only what we want to see.

It is a rare person who can reserve judgement until the last page is turned. Even then, we must rely on the "Faith of our Fathers" to be tolerant enough to understand that many times there are extenuating circumstances which affect each human being on this earth a different way."

Joanne D'Alton Clancy

Sometimes we can't, but if we can - WE HAVE TO TRY!!

CHAPTER EIGHTEEN
CELEBRATE! CELEBRATE!

It is with great enthusiasm that I write this chapter because I love a good party. This whole idea is a throwback to my youth where....Sorry, I digress.

There is always that one parent in the classroom who loves to bake and can be depended upon to masterfully create that special cake for any and all occasions. In my last junior class, I became very dependent upon a particular mom who was gifted in the art of designing all occasion cakes.

She piped out Ghosts and Goblins, Batman and Winnie the Pooh and my all-time favorite, Strawberry Shortcake. (The character) Mrs. Stratton's cakes were always a picture perfect effort and the bonus was that they tasted good too **and** they were always large enough to feed the entire class with just enough left over to send a couple of pieces down to the office. (Get those brownie points whenever you can) As luck would have it, most of my principals were blessed with a sweet tooth and really appreciated the "sugar fix" in their day.

It only takes about fifteen minutes to cut, serve and scarf down a "celebration" cake and you've had a party. I believe that each child in the classroom is worth at least one cake per year. Your job is to find out what kind of cake they've earned.

"Catch 'em doing something right. Reinforce all successful behavior and acknowledge students' efforts."

Some ideas for our celebration cakes were:

1) a hockey player who is **playing** successfully, not necessarily MVP or part of a winning team
2) a child who helped his dad to deliver a new calf (farm country - we get bonus good deeds)
3) a student who **competed** in the festival (dance, singing, drama, instrumental and lived!)

Let's face it! Competing alone is worth the cake and sometimes you can lump a few competitors' accomplishments into one cake. I'm sure that you've caught the idea and can come up with a few "cake ideas' of your own.

I've had to buy a few Sara Lee cakes in a pinch and the chocolate with the chocolate frosting goes over very well.

Birthdays are a wonderful excuse to celebrate. If you are lucky enough to teach Primary, (and I say this with total respect) mothers generally tend to bring in enough treats for the whole class and then some. I brought a huge slab cake into my daughter's Grade 8 Science class on her thirteenth birthday. It was a big hit! I'm sure that one of the reasons was that it took up about fifteen minutes of the lesson and threw a little wrench into the teacher's plan for the period. Kids love that disruption. It makes them feel powerful.

I have always had a snack drawer in my filing cabinet. It comes in handy when you forget your lunch or you can help to subsidize the lunch of the child whose new , "starving" puppy scarfed down a good part of his at the bus stop. Birthday girls and boys, a child who has suffered a serious "owie" on the playground, or that eager helper child who cleaned the blackboard in time for the next class can all benefit from your stash.

My snack drawer has housed a complete spectrum of sweet delights ranging from milk to dark chocolate bars (the Hallowe'en size are the best) to lollipops and bulk barn specials. By following that Girl Guide motto "Be prepared", you always have a prize in your possession. Prizes are given to children who fulfill all types of criteria. I have helpers for everything and can't remember the last time I carried a box out to my car. Again, be creative!

Many of my past students continue to visit and they always enjoy a little treat from the drawer. Hey! Maybe that's why I have so many regular visitors.

SPOIL-ME-DAYS

I don't know who the actual inventor of spoil-me-days was but once I was introduced to them, I was hooked and they immediately became part of my curriculum.

As you may have possibly figured out by now, one of my greatest desires is to inspire my students to read. I tend to obsess on the topic of reading because it is of utmost importance.

My practice is to assign one Book Report to be completed each month. The book must fulfill certain criteria and the Book Report must be complete and accurate. I give a due date and the entire class must have it handed in on that day. When the final, correctly completed report is handed in on time, the class celebrates the following morning or afternoon with a spoil-me-day, which is actually a half day but let's not get too picky. **Be sure that your school has the appropriate permit for viewing movie videos.**

I choose a movie appropriate to the theme or unit that I am teaching. (Could be literature, history, science, etc.) For example, we watched "A Knight's Tale" for the unit on Castles, Knights and their History. Always preview the movie the night before to be sure that there are no questionable scenes or "surprises" for the age group that you teach. It could prove embarrassing if you don't. Again, learn from my experience and trust me. You think that you remember the whole movie and that it will be fine. WRONG!

Students bring snacks and drinks and we do the theater "stuff your face and enjoy" thing. You are utilizing another medium to teach your subject area and they are enjoying a morning of viewing pleasure. It's a win win situation and you get to partake of a veritable smorgasbord of snacks. (One of the reasons that I love to celebrate pretty much anything)

Follow up discussions are invaluable and motivation levels rise. (as my weight has since these "days" have been implemented into my program).

STUDENT OF THE WEEK

Everyone loves to be a star and children are no exception. Every classroom has a bulletin board waiting to be filled. One of ours is always designated for Student of the Week. This allows you to celebrate approximately 34 students per year.

Keep a class list handy to check off each student as they are chosen for the Board. Be sure not to repeat any child. (That defeats the purpose) Be creative and **find a reason for each and every child to be honored on the Board.**

Announce your winner on Friday in order for them to have the weekend to compile a series of photographs for the Board. Pictures should include family members, pets, outings and/or favorite places.

Limit them to about five or six and "guard them with your life" when they are put on the Board. You could even assign a Bulletin Board "police" to patrol and protect. I have had an over zealous boy secretly swipe the photograph of a secret love from "the Board" and it's loss became a very traumatic experience for the victim. Luckily, it was returned.

Find a keen artist in the class to make up large Name Tags or Name Headings for each student and then use the chosen one each week to head up the display. On Monday morning, the new arrangement is tacked up and the last week's winner stands in front of the class to provide explanations of the photos that he/she contributed to the Board. It is an easy, comfortable oral presentation which could be evaluated if you are marking all oral work. Students know the material and are quite comfortable and animated when sharing this information. After they have presented their display, DON'T FORGET TO REWARD THEM WITH A TREAT. A celebration has been created in their honor and they'll remember it for a long time. (In some cases; years)

I have a lifelong friend who loves to celebrate with me. She builds me up and makes me feel special all the time. Often, when we are discussing life's challenges, she'll smile and say, "I think we need to go out and buy a present for you." We hop into the car and head to the nearest shopping mall in search of just the right pick me up. It's amazing some of the things that we have crammed into her car. (Chaise lounges don't fit into the back seat of an Intrepid but...) Over the years, we have faced many life-changing experiences together and have always been there for each other. During university years, my arrival at Barb's door at 6:00 a.m. with coffee and doughnuts was not uncommon and, to this day, my overnight bag is always in the trunk of the car whenever I stop by. For years, she struggled as a single mom and we shared many tears and frustrations. Through it all, our friendship has remained solid and enduring. I believe that one of the main reasons for this is that we always found cause to celebrate. Through the rough times, we looked for little things to celebrate. When things got a little easier, we celebrated. No matter how small the event, we celebrated. Our past is filled with memorable milestones and celebrations. Life has become much better and easier for both of us and still, we celebrate!

Was it always expensive? Not at all! Is it invaluable? You betcha!

*"EVERYTHING WE DO IS AN ATTEMPT TO FEEL GOOD
ABOUT WHO WE ARE, OR WHAT WE ARE GOING
THROUGH"*

Winspiration

CHAPTER NINETEEN
ACCENTUATE THE POSITIVE

I am a motivational speaker and my card reads "Learn With Hearn". You may wonder where I came up with that catchy little title. There is a distinct story there and I wish to share it with you because it clearly outlines the positive impact that one influential person made upon my life.

When I became a teacher for the Lincoln County Board of Education in 1975, we had individual consultants for different subject areas. Yes, this was the dinosaur age. It became fairly obvious that music would become my dominant subject area. When I joined the team of teachers at Queen Mary Junior High School, I was hired to teach music on rotary to approximately 420 students. I needed help!

Having taught music to senior students at my previous school placement, I learned that, generally speaking, pubescent teenage boys would rather chew tin foil than participate positively in any type of music class or choir. Besides, in their girl-oriented brains, it didn't score any points with their really "cool" counterparts who expected them to be all muscle and no wimpiness. (At the age of fourteen, they still had a lot of "muscles yet to create" so wimpiness could not be tolerated even a little bit) They had obviously never seen Grease at that point and still had a lot to learn about what "cool" was.

Many of these "macho wanna-bes" did however, feel that it was going to place them at the epitome of "coolness" if they disrupted the class by croaking off key, farting their insides out and belching on cue. This would definitely raise their status in the dating possibilities of the girls who would roll their eyes and plug their noses, ready for the next onslaught of gastric explosions.

Yes, welcome to the world of Grade 8.

I had, of course, changed that whole scenario at the last school but was now facing the new challenge of adding at least 150 new boys to my list. One of these "growing experiences" was an all boy class of 35 known as 8F. I'm not sure what the "F" actually stood for but I was given quite a few ideas over the course of the year. These boys came in all shapes and sizes, from all walks of life and cultures with an interest in music that ranked at approximately the same level as a tree frog. Each year, there would be an 8F class for me to look forward to. It was now a part of my life and I had to learn to deal with it rather than just tough it out for one year.

So here I was, twenty-four years of age, long blonde hair down my back, a product of a loving, nurturing home environment - the perfect tough girl image that would straighten these boys out and cause them to listen and pay attention. I panicked and called my music consultant, the great and wise Henry Goerzen.

I believe that he was fairly amused when I first called him. I had replaced the veritable genius of a music teacher who was a very large, commanding individual with years of experience under his belt. He had won over the masses, been well-respected and moved on to secondary school to wield his magic there. His death, a few years later, was a significant loss to our Board.

Yes, I was standing in the footprints of Gulliver himself and crying out for help, experiencing a strange mixture of fear and excitement at the possibilities in store.

We all have someone we look up to

Henry became my mentor. He never once caused me to feel inadequate. I did that all by myself. He always spoke positively, providing much needed support. He made me feel that I could accomplish anything that I set out to do. Each time I called the Board Office (and it was often), his secretary, who recognized my voice immediately, would say, "It's Ingrid" and I would hear his voice in the background,

"Is that my talented Buffi girl?" (My maiden name. - Live with that in a senior school. Miss Buffi was not my stage name as I explained to many of the parents that I interviewed over the years.) No matter how frustrated I was or how difficult the challenge, those words, followed by a workable solution to my problem, gave me the strength of a musical Hercules. I invited him to the school often as I had a minimum of 5 choirs practicing during a term. I was always amazed at the control that he wielded and the inspiration he gave to my students. I would sit at the piano and accompany him as he conducted my well-rehearsed students to greater achievements in tone, harmony and obvious enjoyment.

We took many first place trophies and banners back to our school that year and I decided to set a much larger goal for myself. I was going to create two new choirs - a boys ensemble and a school choir of no less than 100 students. I had carried 60 up until now, (10 of which were boys) but it was time to expand my horizons. I didn't share that personal goal with anyone because I was afraid that I would not be able to accomplish it, but I wrote it down and I read it constantly.

Here is where I accidentally learned about the power of the subconscious mind. I kept visualizing my boys' choir winning a trophy. I could see those "tough" boys performing on the risers and I began dreaming about it on a regular basis. I had no other life at the time, no husband in sight and certainly no serious concerns over housework or cooking. One day, I trusted Henry enough to let him in on my secret goal and he became my greatest advocate. Together, we created a History of Rock Unit. He supplied the resources and I wrote up lesson plans and units with accompanying records. (Yes, records!) I created tape recordings of various bands and played them during my note taking classes. Daily music classes became more interesting and fun - something that I hadn't really thought of when it came to learning. My boys reacted much more positively and actually began to learn and enjoy the otherwise tolerated music class.

There was still one very defiant boy who gave me grief. "Music is a waste of time. It's a stupid subject."

I'm not sure if that was a direct quote but it sure sounded like that. He dug in his heels and refused to pass music. In my naivety, I went through the whole process of explaining the importance of a good education and how music incorporates many different subject areas valuable to learning yada yada yada... As I watched his eyes roll into the back of his head, I grasped the realization that none of this mattered to him. The only thing he cared about was basketball. He LOVED basketball. Basketball was his life.

Learn to make Deals

I decided to play "Let's Make a Deal". I appealed to his love of the game and his vanity by inquiring about its rules, plays and tournaments because I was totally basketball illiterate. It seemed to be a pleasure for "Fred" to discuss the game and to describe his favorite sport in such a detailed, interesting way. With the realization that I could become a basketball coach one day, (the thought of new horizons always looms in the distance when you teach and the probability of coaching any sport becomes a very real possibility) I began to take quite an interest in this game. We began to develop quite a rapport he and I, and I attended all of his games, often sitting with his very proud mother who never missed a game. Fred was shorter than all of the other players, but he had a drive to excel and a burning desire to perform well thus, making him a star player. We began a silent pact and music class became a much more comfortable stress-free place when 8F was there. The other boys on the team reaped the benefits as well because I cheered them all on. Miraculously, 8F began to excel in music and, eventually, we created a "rock" performing style that led to an all-boy choir which included Fred. Over time and reputation, my boys' choir became a popular club and we went on to win the approval of many audiences.

I did not see Fred for many years. One day, his sister and I crossed paths. As fate sometimes plays wonderful tricks, she remembered Miss Buffi (she too, had thought it was my stage name)

We discussed Fred and his love for basketball. He had played throughout high school but had developed a new path for his career. She seemed very excited as she disclosed the fact that he was presently a drummer in a jazz band. I went to see Fred play and was terribly moved when I learned that he had his drum inscribed with the words "Be the best that you can be -Buffi".

Never underestimate the power of belief nor its results. **If you believe it, you can achieve it.** But, I digress.

I continued at Queen Mary School and, in my last year there, I was married. My new last name was Hearn and this seemed to amuse my mentor. We had become good friends and I truly loved the man who had given so much of himself to make me feel important. Now when I called, I would hear his voice yell "Is that my favorite Learn with Hearn girl?"

Everything about Henry was positive! His smile, his welcoming personality, his support during festival preparations and his unlimited amount of energy which he gave freely and as often as he could.

A few years later, while teaching at a school specializing in teaching teenagers with disabilities, a group of very enthusiastic singers wished to compete at the Kiwanis Music Festival but there was no appropriate classification for this group. I called Henry. Within a week, he had created a new classification and notified me that we were entered along with two other groups. We competed and won second place "fair and square". One of my students went up to receive the well-earned plaque and banner. That was over 14 years ago. I still meet this girl in my travels and she always reminds of that time "we won, Mrs. Hearn - remember? - we won!"

Upon his retirement, he continued to conduct adult choirs and spread his joy everywhere. Everyone in this area knows Henry and the impact that he has made for hundreds like me. Henry has a zest for life that can not be easily compared to others in his position. I have found that many consultants, administrators and superintendents do not share the dedication of building people up and actually reaching out to those of us who teach. They are often figureheads or sources of information who become unapproachable and difficult to "pin down" for advice and counseling. Sometimes, you're almost afraid to admit that you can't do something or that you need help.

That has been my experience from time to time and, unfortunately, it's reality. It is my firm belief that no matter who you are or what you have achieved, you should still realize that, in this profession especially, we should always work together to be the best we can be.

Our job - our role in life - is to build one another - to lift and truly care for those around us in whatever way we are able.

Henry Goerzen did that for me and for many others. He left a legacy that will live on long after he leaves this planet. I will personally always remember the gift of encouragement and human kindness that he bestowed on me. Wouldn't you like to be remembered in that way?

Planning to be a leader?

If you are considering the role of vice-principal, principal or other administrative titles, always remember this:

A leader serves those whom he/she leads.

I was privileged to work with a wonderful principal who served her teachers. Cathy would regularly volunteer to come into the classroom and teach in order to provide well-deserved breaks or report card "time". Her door was always open and, even though the news was not always what she wanted to hear, it was dealt with in a supportive, constructive manner. Her staff respected her decisions which were generally made after consultation with them. Everyone worked harder and more creatively because she allowed them the "freedom" to do their job.

I have a great respect for leaders who are a part of a team rather than the dominant factors who try to run everything. As a leader, you will earn the love and respect of your peers by being a positive, supportive team player. You will earn resentment, anger and poor results if you try to control and impose your opinions and rules upon the team you feel is beneath you.

It's your choice. Make it wisely.

"WHEN YOU PUT FENCES AROUND PEOPLE, YOU GET SHEEP"

Anonymous

Make Valuable Impressions - They make Memories

Children almost always remember their primary, junior and intermediate teachers. They know them by name and the various categories assigned to them... breath on a scale of 1-10, hairdo and its relationship to fashion, type of clothes, shoe size and so on. Somehow, it has become a statistic that elementary teachers hit the "memory zone" much more often than secondary teachers and even university professors. I have interviewed hundreds of people, including many my age and have found, surprisingly enough, that the large majority remembers the grades 1-8 teachers much more vividly than those who taught these individuals in the following years.

Generally speaking, if you are not a rotary teacher, you will spend almost 10 months out of a year with children in your class. Your face will greet them each time they enter your homeroom; morning recess, after lunch, returning from assemblies, etc. You will have seen their faces during the years before you taught them and the years after if all of you remain in the same school. You are in the process of marking their lives with indelible ink. Your soft clucks and coos will be their beacon of comfort when sporting an injury or playground war wound. It's you that they'll turn to when they are facing a life changing problem or, better yet, a victory! How will you be remembered?

Shopping for groceries, I ran into a student whom I had taught 22 years before. She spotted me out of the corner of her eye, yelled my name and ran over to give me a hug, leaving her two year old son unattended in the shopping cart. (He was actually in full view the entire time). Twenty years before, she had moved away, eventually met her husband and took up residence in Parry Sound. I hadn't seen or heard from her in all of that time. I can't even begin to explain what a thrill it was for me to know that she felt comfortable enough to attack me in public with a hug!

I am noted for my hugs. I have experienced six foot four inch boys hug me at the mall and am shocked to find how quickly they have reached 25 years of age.

My motto has always been "If I can no longer hug children, I will no longer teach." I have hugged thousands of children in my life and am grateful for having had the opportunity to show them that little gesture of love; the true feeling that I had inside for them. People who don't know and understand me may think that there are "ulterior motives" for my hugging children, but quite honestly, I have rarely encountered a student who would turn down a hug when being comforted or congratulated. They get it! My friends, family and I do it all the time.

I guess there is that question of what's acceptable to a child, and quite honestly, I have made this statement at the beginning of each new school year. I say it in such a way that there is no immediate reaction required, but there is an awareness of alternative behaviors.

"If you don't like being hugged, I respect that. It is my way of showing you how much I care. If you do not wish to be hugged, please let me know at some convenient time and I will certainly respect your wishes."

In all of my twenty-eight years of teaching with the Board, only one boy came to me after I had made "my statement" and asked not to be hugged. It made him feel uncomfortable and I was fully aware that there could be children who did not like hugs. There was nothing more said and the year was spent in alternative forms of praise. This boy exceeded many of his own expectations that year and, upon winning the Ontario Scholar's award, on stage, in front of the entire audience of parents and students, hugged me when presented with his medal. I don't know who was more shocked, he or I, but it was a memorable moment for both of us.

CHAPTER TWENTY

TRAGEDY IN THE CLASSROOM

One of my greatest fears has always been the possibility of losing one of my students through an accident or illness. It was such a great fear that I blocked it from my mind, the hope that I would never need a plan of action.

In June of 2000, I applied for a new position with the Board thinking that my five years at my present school were up and it was time to move on. As usual, I looked for something totally different and found a posting in the special education resource department, a position that I was qualified for and felt that I would enjoy. With great confidence, I applied and followed up with the interview. During the interview, I began to feel unsure about my abilities. I had become quite emotional when answering one of the questions and had rambled. Me - I had rambled - very hard to believe...

A very kind superintendent called me at home to inform me that, although she felt that I had many wonderful attributes, my answers were too long. Due to the number of talented people applying for the position, that flaw took me out of the running. She spent some time on the phone rebuilding some of the confidence and self esteem that had crumbled moments before and then allowed me to deal with it.

I won't tell you that I was not upset because I was. I went through the whole process of "why didn't I say this?" and "how could I have said that"; you know the drill. We think of all the right answers and reactions after it's over.

I do that all the time, especially when I need a quick comeback. I find some lame thing to say and then go through an entire list of Martin Scorsese comebacks an hour later when it doesn't matter. It's only me and the doughnut having a chat.

Anyway, after beating myself up, I bought a dozen doughnuts (they now have Krispee Kremes in Canada) and reread my Napoleon Hill book from cover to cover.

I returned to school the next day somewhat intact and reported my plans of remaining for another year to my empathetic yet elated principal who had just been relieved of the duty of interviewing music teachers . Two days later, I was fine and in the serious throes of graduation slides, final grad dinner plans and the basic, end of the year roller coaster ride.

With renewed energy and enthusiasm, I faced my 2001 Grade 8 class in September and what a class they were! Thirty three wonderful teenagers, most of whom had grown up together. I could already sense that this was going to be an amazing leadership class as the creativity was very evident from the beginning.

I had taught most of these children music since Grade 4 and knew many of their individual talents. Since the graduating class heads up most of the assemblies, fund-raisers, spirit days and choir presentations, we were in for a "fun" year. A week into school, I had totally forgotten about having applied "out" and was very happy and grateful to be the "leader of the 8 pack." (My MSN handle)

September went very well. This class loved discussions and we had delved into many interesting areas, one of which was UN Debates, a personal favorite. I had some talented math scholars who would make perfect team teaching partners so I felt confident about teaching the program effectively and our wise and all-knowing principal had hired a new intermediate teacher who would deal with the Grade 8 Science program which saved me a lion's share of grief. We were definitely in business and I was pumped!

Near the end of October, one of my bicycle enthusiasts had a very serious accident leaving her with a severely broken shoulder and long-term bed rest. Hallowe'en was just around the corner; Grade 8 Hallowe'en; the last year of trick-or-treating for most of these teens; a major celebration in our town.

Well, the class got together and created a support group who would not go trick-or- treating, but would spend the evening lifting the spirits of their friend. Many of the others, who did collect candy, dropped much of it off to be shared by the group. Everyone was happy with the results and I was touched at the obvious concern and commitment that these children had for one another. They continued in this way. Art class was devoted to creating silly cards of well wishes and children took turns bringing and returning homework assignments which this young lady's mother faithfully oversaw and reinforced at home. This girl received the newsletters, sports info. and all other relevant data for a Grade 8 student to remain in "the Loop".

From all reports and visits, things were copasetic. She was in good spirits and healing well.

A week later, on Sunday evening, I received a phone call from one of the supply teachers in the community. She wished to inform me of a terrible accident and felt that I should be prepared for Monday. The mother of one of my boys had died that morning and the news was moving through town very quickly. I would be walking into a very difficult situation the next day and I needed to be prepared. I immediately called the principal of our school, and we discussed a plan of attack. I received a few more phone calls from concerned parents and had pretty much the whole picture in hand when I reached the school the next morning.

As we sat in her office, Catherine provided both emotional and physical support. She had already called the crisis counselor and we began to plan our strategy. The counselor arrived before the children did so we were as prepared for their questions as we could be at this point.

CHILDREN HAVE A MULTITUDE OF QUESTIONS

It was decided that I would sit alone in front of my class and report the facts as I knew them. Mustering all the courage I could, I began the task of dealing with the situation. As you can imagine, there were already a few versions of the story and I worked hard to clarify, explain and support the questions and concerns of the tear-stained faces in front of me. As soon as the facts were clear, we moved directly into a discussion of this wonderful mother at great length. We discussed all the positive things that she had provided for these children throughout their lives and we began to celebrate her life by sharing these memories. All of this was done with only me in front of the class. It was felt that the children would relate best to their own teacher at this point and no strangers or others were invited in as yet. We passed around Kleenex boxes and allowed tears without judgement. Boys and girls shared stories and tears as they sat in their desks and contributed their experiences and concerns.

The next step was to create a definite, clear plan of dealing with this horrible tragedy. Students began to calm down as they created a list of things that we could do. **Children need concrete plans**. They need a list, a plan of attack, so to speak. It has a calming effect and it reassures them that they can do something. Not only would they become a part of their friend's grief, but also a vital component of his future healing. This process provides a positive focus rather than the negative tossing around of endless thoughts and ideas that would accomplish nothing.

We discussed each concern at length, allowing the children to share their fears and beliefs. **This is no time to avoid religious contributions**. Children have the need to express their beliefs without criticism, shame or ridicule. Each one was given the opportunity to share and we dealt with each issue as a group.

It is important to note that the teacher becomes the mediator. You can tell who is going "over the top", so you deal with each view carefully. Don't stifle, just reroute, and above all,

"Never impose your own religious beliefs upon your students."

Many parents have spent a lifetime instilling personal religious views and beliefs in their children. These children are now very vulnerable. It is not your role to change or try to modify these beliefs in any way. In this particular case, I was dealing mostly with Christian views and shared them as support, not imposition. Yes, there were quiet students who contributed little or nothing but they were still a part of the process and gleaned whatever they wished from their peers.

During this part of the discussion, the counselor had slipped into the room and was there as a listener only. After much conversation, she was introduced and her services were offered to those who felt that they needed special attention.

She then took over the class and shared her expertise with them, again, allowing them to discuss and vent. Only a handful of students accompanied her to the staff room where she met with them individually for a period of time. I remained in the classroom throughout the entire discussion in order to support the class with a familiar "face". I did not attend any private sessions, however, as I may have become an obstacle. We think that children need our love and support but we must also realize that sometimes they may not wish to express honest views and opinions around us. I learned a long time ago that sometimes children need to vent without their teacher in the room and have swallowed enough pride to realize that I can't fix everything, in fact, I could be part of the problem. (Be willing to accept that you can't make everyone happy all of the time and you will be much more able to handle conflict.)

As a class, we continued with our plan. Always allow students to have the choice of participating or not. In this case, they all chose to participate and support their friend but that will not always happen. There may be children who will not wish to be a part of any plans being made. They should, however, be encouraged to listen and respect the others. This, I am told, still allows them to be part of a grieving process that they may not even be aware of needing.

Students then broke into smaller groups and moved about the room, sharing thoughts, feelings, memories and experiences. This mother had been a "hockey mom" and had built close ties with many of the boys in the class. Because her son was so popular and well-liked, a great majority of the students had either met her or spent time in the family's home. I listened to the wonderful stories that the children shared and I soon realized just how close this little community truly was. Every single student in this class was affected by the death of this mother. That, in itself, was a wonderful tribute to her.

Be Flexible Enough to Change Direction Quickly

No school work was done that day. All rotary classes were canceled and I had a two hour art lesson where the students created and cut out houses, horses, people and scenery for "Dickensville". We had been reading "A Christmas Story" by Charles Dickens. It was a story of hope and promise and the students began to focus on their artistic endeavors as they continued to share in a much more settled, focused environment.

By the end of the day, things were calmer and I knew that the parents would now take over the healing process. My greatest challenge had been dealt with and we would carry on. The next day became more normal as children returned to their studies even though we did dedicate one class to completing and reviewing "The Plan".

That evening, students, accompanied by their parents, paid their respects at a very packed, emotion-filled funeral home and they had the opportunity of visiting with their friend. Many of the boys had already created a schedule where the young man would be visiting with them, joining them for dinner and even staying overnight. He would not be returning to school for two weeks and each day was planned out. Each of his good friends would miss a day of school to spend with him. This was a good part of the plan and certainly not a difficult one to accommodate.

Our class plan was set out in a distinct list.

(1) Visitation

There was visitation at the funeral home. This was a very individual part of the plan. Those who wished to visit the funeral home did so with their parents or their friends. It was a separate part of the class plan. This was left up to the individual student and it became a more comfortable decision for each child to make. No one would actually know who did or did not visit and no one would have to explain. For some children, it was too traumatic to deal with.

(2) Contributions of Food

Food is always a topic for discussion and it was decided that we could bake. This young man and his father loved baked goods so we created a "baking" calendar. Each Friday, two students would bring in a few homemade treats for him. They would be taken home for the weekend and he and his dad would enjoy a few goodies from his friends. Almost every child signed up for a week in the calendar year and many signed up for two. This worked very well and we provided baked goods until the last day of school. I know that he appreciated the thought and concern from his fellow peers and expressed this a few times throughout the year.

(3) The Funeral Itself

The class plan had put us all together as a well-dressed, respectful group walking to the local church at 10:30 a.m. There were four full pews saved for us and we were escorted into them. The Grade 8s exemplified dignity and respect for their friend and his family. They opted to return to the school for lunch and spend the time together rather than attend the luncheon provided. I was so proud of them that my heart was full and I spent the evening weeping at the realization that I had almost missed the opportunity of teaching this fine group of young people.

The boys systematically took a day off to spend with their buddy and parents provided activities and meals to get him through this difficult time. After two weeks, he returned to class.

I have to mention one of my amazing, talented students. She decided to compose and perform a song for her friend. It was a beautiful tribute to the friendship that he had in his classmates. It gave him reassurance that he would never be alone. Thank you Violet, for that inspiration.

The next few weeks brought normality back into the classroom. Choir practices prepared us for our school musical, sports programs revealed the talents of winning teams and, once again, our group was together. Our cyclist had returned, our courageous young man returned to his hockey team and it seemed as though things were going to be fine. Each Thursday, a group of us met at the arena to cheer the hockey team on as they sped across the ice, sticks slapping against the puck causing great roars of excitement. I had never taken a real interest in hockey but over the last few years, I was learning and "my kids" were teaching me to stay calm whenever there was a "confrontation" or other exciting moment which involved possible harm to one of "my boys."

Towards the end of November, I noticed that one of my brightest lights in the classroom was suffering quite a bit with the flu. Rebecca was a very academic, athletic girl who maintained very high standards for herself and was quite concerned about missing school. She tried to attend but was becoming weaker and more nauseated as the days went by.

Rebecca was six feet tall and a star volleyball and basketball player. She was a voracious cheerleader and a firm supporter of her friends. Rebecca believed very strongly that "if you can't say something good, don't say anything at all." She was the epitome of an all round, multi-faceted student who exhibited all of the best qualities of both sportsmanship and citizenship. It was under her direction that we had created the successful "plan" that was so bravely and perfectly executed for her classmate.

I needed her to know that her health was much more important than her schoolwork. When her dad came to pick her up after a very upsetting episode in the washroom, it was agreed that she would not return until she was well. We would not worry about the academics; she had already exceeded the expectations for this Grade level and it was only the end of November. With a final drawn out, tearful hug, I sent her home.

My own child had suffered with "mono" the year before and I was almost convinced that this young girl was struggling with the same symptoms and illness. Her parents had been to their doctor a number of times but this time, they took her directly to the hospital for tests.

That evening, I received a call from her mom acknowledging that she did, indeed, have mono but that they were sending her to the McMaster Health Sciences Hospital in Hamilton for more extensive blood work because something was still unclear.

The next day, Friday, at 3:45 p.m. I received a phone call that would change my life forever. Rebecca, my Rebecca, my wonderful, perfect student had been diagnosed with a very aggressive form of leukemia and would begin chemotherapy treatment the next day.

There are no words that can adequately describe the anguish that I felt. I know that it took a long time for me to compose myself enough to walk down to the office. Together, my principal and I shared our emotions and the total unreality of the situation. There were too many questions and we knew that, on Monday morning, we would once again have to face the Grade 8 class with difficult news. We were told that no one would know until after it was announced on Monday. The family, in their wisdom and compassion for our students would keep the information to themselves until we prepared the children.

The enormity of the task ahead sat like a lead weight in the pit of my stomach. My own daughter is named Rebecca. She is one year younger than Rebecca Plett and I can't even begin to explain how much more precious she has become to me. This was her friend too and I struggled with the task of finding a way to handle this situation on Monday, both as a parent and as a teacher.

Once again, the crisis counselor was called in and once again, I faced an incredibly courageous class. They knew instinctively that something was wrong when I walked in as we had bonded and almost become related during these last few weeks. I had not stopped crying all weekend and couldn't even begin to imagine the horror that the family was dealing with.

My announcement was as straightforward as I could make it.

"We know that Rebecca has been suffering with the flu and maybe even mono. Her sister called me on Friday to say that she does, in fact, have mono, but that she is also suffering from a serious blood disorder called leukemia." Who was I kidding?

In seconds, students had verified this as cancer and we had to face this head on.

"Is she going to die, Mrs. Hearn?"

This question came from the young man who had recently lost his mom. The look on his face was so intense and so filled with concern that I could hardly speak. As I write this chapter, I can see it so clearly that I am overcome with emotion.

"No one knows yet how serious it is. They are beginning treatments. It has been cured in children before. Remember Josh? He had leukemia and has been in remission for eight years. He's leading a normal life again and is skateboarding with the rest of his friends. We hope that this will be the case with Rebecca too."

I have seen the faith of children many times throughout my life - faith that their team can win, faith that they will pass a test, faith in the weather - but I have never in my life seen the combined group's faith in God as I saw it that day. One of the girls asked if we could hold hands and pray. I know for a fact that there were some children in that classroom who had never attended a church service or even knew what a serious prayer was but every single student joined hands with another and we prayed. One student began and another would continue until the room was totally quiet. We do not repeat the Lord's Prayer in our public schools but this group of overwhelmed, faithful children believed that they needed to call upon a Force much greater than ours to help their friend and to help us through yet another crisis. This was the beginning of our journey and Christmas was three weeks away.

Once again, it was time to create a plan

The first thing that we decided to do was to leave Rebecca's desk totally intact. No one would use it or remove her things from it. It would sit unoccupied as a silent reminder that she was still very much a part of our class and in our thoughts. Anything that was handed out was put on her desk as well. All papers would be compiled and put into a folder for her parents. This was done faithfully and worked out very well. The children continued to think of her as a student who was just absent and it helped them deal with this crisis in a more normal way. I believe that this made a big difference in their ability to move forward.

A bulletin board was dedicated to Rebecca. It was the "Becka Board". Each month, a huge calendar was created by two different students. It was colorful and bright reflecting her favorite colors and sayings. Photographs of Rebecca were tacked on and around it. We were told that we could begin visiting her at the hospital so students could sign up for Tuesday and Thursday nights making teams of four for each visit. Parents were notified of our plans and began volunteering to drive the one hour distance to and from the hospital on these nights. It was amazing to see the number of volunteers that signed up to drive and support our efforts. We were a team and we were on a mission. The calendar became the focal point in providing information for the Pletts. All activities and events were written on the correct days and children began writing inspirational comments and greetings all over it. At the end of each month, the calendar was carefully removed, folded and added to the pile of things being delivered to the hospital. The calendars were hung on the wall of Rebecca's hospital room as a constant reminder that she was in our thoughts and part of our class. Her room became a bit cluttered, but it was "good clutter" and helped to keep her spirits up. This was a very useful tool in allowing all children to be a part of her world.

Our Plan continues

Our class had been practicing for the Christmas concert and we had a virtual plethora of Christmas songs available. A mini choir was created and we scheduled a performance at the hospital the Friday before the holidays. Our plans were to sing in the playroom in order that other patients would be able to enjoy our musical talents as well.

It was a devastating blow to learn that Rebecca would not be able to have visitors after all. She had suffered a major setback, an infection, and visitors were not allowed. Eventually, she fell into a coma (I believe that it was induced to help her to heal) and we now had to wait for further news. Luckily, the Christmas holidays were fast approaching and the children had something else to occupy their minds. Christmas cards and letters were sent to the hospital along with many prayers of hope for Rebecca's recovery.

They returned with renewed energy after the holidays and decided to prepare for the time that they would be able to once again visit. The most amazing thing that I experienced was that these children were able to concentrate on their class work and actually achieve successes in school. Because they were doing everything that they could for Rebecca, there was little guilt and they were able to continue on with their own lives as well. Sometimes, when discussions focused on the question, "Why did Rebecca get sick and not one of us?", we had to deal with the fact that it would have been just as devastating for any child to become ill and we really had no answers as to who is chosen and why. My prime purpose was to relieve them of the guilt of not being ill themselves. It was astounding how many of them felt that they would rather have been sick themselves than to see their friend so ill. Trying to relieve their guilt was a very important component of the coping process.

Through all of this they headed up Spirit Days, sports assemblies and talent shows. They included comments about Rebecca whenever it was appropriate and continued to make her a vital part of the Grade 8 class. The staff and students were very supportive in accepting all comments and tributes that the Grade 8 class made. Everyone "was on board." We included the whole junior and senior division in our activities of signing cards and sending notes. Those who wished to contribute were welcomed and became part of the process.

The Grade 8 class formed a collective group who physically displayed their support and prayers by wearing a yellow arm band. These were provided and given out freely by the Grade 8s themselves. All students in the junior and senior division who wished to participate wore them. Some of the staff wore them as well. They were sported every day, all day, in public and in private. They were a constant reminder that we were thinking and praying for our friend. The entire community became very aware of the support of the children as they saw the arm bands at grocery stores, sports activities, hockey games...

Rebecca was a lover of cows. As a result, a multitude of cows began to enter the school. There were cow socks and cow slippers, stuffed cows and cups with cows, cow cards and cow well wishes. All arrived at the school to be delivered during our upcoming visits. School notes and memorabilia were sent to the family on a regular basis. Mrs. Plett informed me that this was very important to her because it kept her in touch with the things that were going on at the school. It gave her some feeling of belonging and not being totally apart from us. We tried very hard to keep Rebecca's family as much a part of our program and activities as we could even though Mr. and Mrs. Plett lived in Hamilton most of the time. There were always phone calls to keep us informed and they were truly exemplary in making us a part of Rebecca's life throughout this whole ordeal.

We were allowed to once again resume visiting in February and put our calendar into full swing. Students took turns signing up to visit the two days each week. We would wait for phone calls that would give permission to come. Bad weather hit once or twice but most of the time, the visits went well. Rebecca's fourteenth birthday was celebrated on Valentine's Day.

Children directed and produced humorous videos which they left for Rebecca to watch throughout the day when they were not there. These videos were filled with greetings and humor. Rebecca reported that she enjoyed these so much because she would play them over and over to feel close to her friends.

I remember one of our visits that turned into a talent show. Each of the girls entertained Rebecca in the play room while she sat in her wheelchair. There were a few piano solos, a musical voice number, some dancing and the telling of bad jokes.

Sometimes we were allowed to take Rebecca on a wheelchair ride out to the patio and I believe that she really enjoyed getting outside with her friends and expressing her true feelings and thoughts.

Throughout all of this, Rebecca remained strong and full of the faith that she would return to her class. She sent e-mails through her wonderful sisters and sent messages of faith and courage to each of us. The girls would bring in notes and letters that they had received from their friend. We would read them to the class and spend time each day to discuss Rebecca. Her family members went above and beyond the call of duty by informing us of each and every step of her struggles. She remained strong and resolute in overcoming this serious illness.

There were many pitfalls, many disappointments, but through it all, her main focus was that she was going to attend graduation. Her room was filled with gifts and thoughts from her many friends; their support, love and prayers were evident everywhere and they were going to help her through this. Even the nursing staff encouraged us and praised us for our efforts, giving the children hope and renewed energy to think positively and keep going.

I cannot describe Rebecca's condition during this time. To see a disease ravage a child's body in such a catastrophic way is unbelievable. As a mother, I could hardly deal with the visits, let alone the ongoing care and endless support that this loving mother provided on an everyday basis. She remained strong and positive, always greeting us with a smile and a hug, leaving us with words of encouragement. She and I both realized just what a special group of young people we were dealing with and she was always grateful for their continuous love and support.

I remember one particular night. We had decided to have a pajama party in Rebecca's room. Eight girls, a fellow teacher and myself dressed in pajamas and headed out to the hospital on a Friday evening. We looked pretty strange coming in wearing our "jammies" and clutching stuffed toys and snacks. Rebecca missed her pajama parties so it was decided to have one with her at the hospital. Even though she slept through quite a bit of the movie, I know that it meant a lot to her to have us there. Remember - be willing to take reasonable risks - even if you look a little funny - it's well worth the results and you make memories.

Each day, we set aside a few minutes to discuss Rebecca. Sometimes it was to share a poem or letter she had written, sometimes to vent about this terrible illness that was controlling her life. We needed to have a "Rebecca time" each day in order to get on with the every day school work that needed to be done. After these few minutes, we were much more able to resume our daily schedule.

Rebecca did attend graduation in June. With the help of her parents and family, nurses and ambulance, she was able to be home for a short while. Her mother sewed her a beautiful, pastel green, long gown, her wig was youthful and set with tiny flowers and she was wheeled in to join her friends at the ceremony.

I couldn't contain my emotion as she was presented with the "Spirit Award" which she so justly had earned over her years at Virgil and especially this year. Her mother stood in front of the entire student body and guests to publicly thank all of those who had been providing so much support over the last few months.

The class picture was complete when taken outside and the graduates were filled with pride as they watched their friend being

195

wheeled through the crowd. They were so proud of her courage and faith and they loved her so much. We had come to the end of the most memorable and fulfilling years of my entire career...and to think, I could have missed it by leaving. I realize and believe that I was meant to stay that year because I had known those children for quite a long time and was able to be a part of that life-changing experience. What had begun as a disappointment became a truly unique life-changing experience for me and I was very grateful for the opportunity to have been the "leader of the 8 pack".

Rebecca passed away peacefully on Thursday, September 28th, surrounded by her family singing her favorite songs at her bedside. News got out pretty quickly and bereavement counselors were available at the three high schools affected on Friday morning.

The girls began arriving at our school by 2 p.m. Friday afternoon and congregated in the staff room. There were brightly colored blank pages with the heading "Special Memories..." and each child was encouraged to recount a memorable time they had spent with Rebecca or some wonderful memories that they had to share. These pages were later bound together in coordination with the other schools as a booklet and given to Mrs. Plett as a reminder of how much Rebecca was loved and would be missed.

By 4p.m., most of the girls joined me in walking to a local restaurant for pizza and grieving. After dinner, we continued our journey to the house of our "cyclist" whose mother had generously opened her home to the group for the entire evening. We spent hours discussing feelings, good and bad memories of the past year's ordeal and future plans. We sat at the piano and sang some favorite songs from our repertoire the year before. We laughed and cried, sharing openly and honestly. I would say that this was one of the more important parts of the healing process and many of the girls received their closure during this wonderful meeting time. We planned our contributions for both the funeral and the memorial service which, it was decided would be hosted and implemented by the graduating class. The boys did not attend this meeting, not because they weren't invited, but because they chose to deal with it in their own way. At least two of them went home to compose a letter of sympathy to the Plett family.

Her funeral, held on the following Monday was attended by almost all of the graduating class. A group of her friends practiced one of her favorite songs, A Child's Prayer, during the lunch hour and performed it as part of the program. Again, special seating was arranged for the entire group and we sat as a class; our special class.

The new principal to our school was incredibly supportive and helpful in every way as we organized a memorial service at our school which, again, almost all of the graduating class attended. It was an extremely emotional sight to watch them assemble, wearing their yellow arm bands in a final tribute to their friend. The gymnasium was filled by those children from the junior and senior grades who wished to attend as well as many community members. The Pletts are a popular family in the community and it was wonderful to see the support given to them at this time. Mrs. Plett has been a teacher at a nearby school for many years and has taught many of the children in the area. Five Plett children have been a part of our school system.

We read stories, poems and recited memories of this wonderful Virgil graduate who had only been on this earth for fourteen years. Once again, our talented composer, vocalist and pianist performed her own personally written song of remembrance for Rebecca. I enlisted the help of past students to play instruments for our musical numbers and we videotaped the entire service to give to the Plett family as a lifelong memory.

Rebecca Plett has left a legacy that will go on in our community for many more years. She has set a wonderful example for our students to follow.

As a final tribute, our school community collected money and purchased a Trisha Romance painting aptly named "Faithful Friends". With the generosity of the Preservation Gallery, we were able to present a huge framed picture to the family at our Christmas program that December. A great majority of the class stood on the bleachers to present this gift to the Plett family. On the back are hundreds of signatures of students and parents who wished to sign and pay tribute to Rebecca Plett, a child who gave so much in such a very short time. The school has created a "Rebecca Plett Spirit Award" which will be presented each year to a student who exhibits great school spirit and support to their peers. It is twinned with a financial gift that has been generously donated by Mr. and Mrs. Plett.

I will always be grateful for the strength, courage and example that Rebecca shared with us. She was truly a special child who exemplified all of the qualities that a teacher tries to instill in a child. She had those qualities and much more. Thank you Rebecca!!!

I would very much like to thank the Plett family for allowing me to share this story with you. They are indeed a very special family. In February, on Rebecca's birthday, her friends were invited to the Plett home and they celebrated her life, once again sharing and keeping her memory alive. Her friends make every effort to visit and "keep in touch" because they understand how valuable a gift it is for Rebecca's mom.

I hope that you will never have to experience this lesson in your lifetime of teaching but, if you do, know that you will not be alone and that there is a huge support system out there for you. In writing this chapter, I hope that it has provided some guidance and experience.

It has been one of the most important chapters in this book because I know for a surety that I learned much more from these students than they learned from me during this year. My education exceeded my expectations and I am humbled by the overwhelming courage, love and citizenship that was displayed and practiced daily by children; those whom we teach but, more importantly, those who teach us.

I am so grateful to my "kids". You know who you are. You're the best!!!!!

CHAPTER TWENTY-ONE
GO THE EXTRA MILE

It is a very evident phenomena that people who "go the extra mile" are the achievers, the successful handful of society who play by Nature's rules. Life gives back to us exactly what we give.

Sowing the Seed

"Out of the past the present eternally springs,
You may sow what you will but tomorrow will bring
You the harvest to show you the manner of things
Is the seed you have chosen to sow."

New Psychology

I agree with Napoleon Hill who states that "an important principal of success in all walks of life and in all occupations is a willingness to Go the Extra Mile; which means the rendering of more and better service than that for which one is paid, and giving it in a **positive mental attitude**."

If you look at all of the examples of great and successful leaders in business, politics and other careers, you will find this to be a truth.

A PERSONAL NOTE

It is a sad truth that we seldom realize the value of our parent's teachings as we are growing up.

How could they possibly understand "our" generation? They lived in dinosaur time and things were so different then. My children use the same lines on me now and I have to smile as I think of my youth and my inexperienced attitude toward the loving values and important truths that my parents gave me.

My dad was born a German, the only son and brother to one sister. At the age of eighteen, due to the Second World War, he was forced to become a young soldier and, three years later, was taken as a prisoner of war, spending his early twenties in a Russian Prison

Camp. He has recounted many stories of the extra responsibilities that he took on in his platoon of soldiers during those eight years away. By taking on extra work and discovering ingenious ways to attain cigarettes and chocolate for the men, he found favor in the leaders of the Camp and was able to raise himself up to a position of responsibility among the prisoners.

After the dust of war settled, he was one of the few of the original group of young soldiers to return home alive. With no opportunity for education and very little work available, there was not much incentive to stay in his war-torn country, so he packed his bags, said his goodbyes to family and friends and set out on the voyage to Canada, the "land of opportunity and freedom", not knowing what was in store but ready to accept the challenge of a new life.

Having met my mother just three months prior to leaving Germany, he soon wrote her and asked her to join him and be married. She collected her few items of value and crossed the ocean to meet him. They were married in the tiny town of Port Colborne and a new family was born.

Their first child (that would be me) caused them considerable difficulty because I was born with a congenital hip displacement which, at that time, required a very new and expensive procedure in a Toronto hospital. My father, determined to provide the very best care for his first child, worked many hours of overtime and performed odd jobs in order to pay the staggering medical bills. There was no health insurance and he had to bear the burden of these costs or raise a crippled child. To him, there was only one choice and he made it.

I, of course, being a young child, had no idea of what was happening and even forget the memory of that ordeal. My father, on the other hand, lived with the knowledge for the rest of his life, that he had done everything in his power to give his child the very best in medical care, allowing her to grow and play with other children in a normal world. My parents had gone "the extra mile" and it had not been easy. Their determination and sacrifices provided me a lifetime free of a physical disability.

This pair always taught each and every one of their four children that you must always do your best and then a little extra. Never "just finish" the job. Always leave your mark and be proud of your accomplishments. It was the way they lived and they wished to pass that great value on to their children.

I use my dad as an example because it relates to me personally and it personifies the lesson I wish to concentrate on. This man came to Canada as a non English speaking immigrant. He carried with him only a suitcase and a dream. Education had not been possible and the opportunity of a new life became the goal.

The first thing he did was attend school to learn the English language. With the goal of citizenship came the desire to belong and succeed. He was successful in grasping the language and, when I talk to people who knew my dad, they always speak of a man who worked hard and gave the best he had; always. Every job that he took, every task that he fulfilled was done to the best of his ability. He built a reputation for himself which earned him new offers of jobs and small raises. Nothing was "beneath" him and he used each experience as a rung of a ladder to move upward.

As a young girl, I would remember my dad sitting with me to do homework. It was always a mandatory part of the assignment to "add a little bit extra". A picture, a poem, a verse or some bit of trivia would end the project. It had to be neat and clearly written. Pages were sometimes torn from my book as my dad worked to teach us the difference between what was acceptable and what was right.

He and I would often sit at the piano and I would play my selections for the week. He would sing along with them or just listen to make sure that there were no mistakes. When the technical parts were successfully mastered, he would speak of adding "myself to the music". I would try to feel the music as he sat, sometimes for an hour, and coached me along. As a child, I sometimes thought him to be mean and intolerant. I could not understand that he saw talent in his young child and wanted more for her life than the difficulties that he had endured. He especially wanted his children to acquire an education.

My dad drove me to many festivals and competitions that were held in the Niagara Region for many years, instilling a desire to improve and become more confident, performing by competing with others. Through all of this, he taught me to win graciously and to accept defeat without resentment.

"Everyone has to win first place sometimes, you can't always take the prize," he would remind me. He taught me to congratulate the winners and be grateful for the opportunity of competing. When the trophy did not reach my arms, there were few grudges, only fleeting moments of disappointment and then a sense of accomplishment at having tried and been a part of the experience. Over the years, I became friends with some of my competitors and we would sit together and sincerely wish each other luck. With each festival or recital came praise, a mini- celebration (ice cream sundae or other special treat) and the knowledge that my parents were proud of my efforts. My confidence in performing grew and, by the time I reached high school, I knew that I wished to become a music teacher.

My dad worked in factories most of his life and when there were lay-offs, he would find whatever there was out there. He never stopped working for his family and always provided both the necessities and, as we grew older, many luxuries of life. Each of his children were given the opportunity to choose a post-secondary educational facility that they wished to attend and he generously paid for their education. His goal and desire was to provide an education and the opportunity of a life with fewer struggles for his children.

When I review the journey that my mom and dad had together, I can see a pattern of successes that came their way. Life became easier. Brand new cars were purchased and trips were taken. They began dating, (a luxury that they had never really been able to afford when they first came to Canada) driving to other cities for dinner and shopping. My dad had always worked that extra bit to succeed and even though it was never the job that he would have chosen, he always performed his duties to the best of his ability and then some.

The thing that always strikes me is that many parents feel that their obligation to their children is complete when they grow up to, say 21 years of age. Even though I had grown up, there wasn't a Christmas concert or musical that my mom and dad missed in all of the years that he was alive. He would switch shifts with others and he and my mom would always be those special faces in the crowd whenever my choirs performed. That was something that I could always rely on. My mom still, to this day, attends all the performances that I conduct and often will illicit the company of a friend or my own children to sit with her. At my age, it's pretty cool to see my mom sitting in the audience. These are my role models, these are the examples that have taught me this very important philosophy.

I have two sisters and one brother and I am happy to announce that they, too, personify this lesson of going the "extra mile." Each one of them is noted for doing that little bit extra in their place of employment and all of them are happy, successful people.

Years before I met the teachings of Napoleon Hill or Venice Bloodworth, my parents were already teaching me the steps to building success. They were immigrants who knew and lived strong values of accountability and responsibility to each other, to their offspring and families and to Nature itself. I am grateful for these two wonderful teachers in my life and I know that they inspired me to pass their beliefs and strengths on to my own children as well as the children I teach.

ON THE SUBJECT OF PRIDE

"Where, along the way, have so many, and in such a short time, lost their pride in personal accomplishments? And why?

A craftsman or workman used to do his very best so that when his job was finished he could proudly say, "My reputation for good workmanship speaks for itself."

Nowadays it appears to be just the opposite. One contracts for work to be done at home (or anywhere for that matter!) And the results are often shocking.

Your deeds and works live long on after you are gone so why not take pride in all that you do? Never lose sight of the fact that you are an individual who has the power of choice - to lift himself above the herd of humanity or be lost in its crowded maze. Always do the very best work you can, no matter what the job."

Joanne D'Alton Clancy - "a way out from in"

The principle of "going the extra mile" is not man-made. It is a distinct part of Nature's handiwork.

We can observe this principle in the production of food that grows from the soil, where the farmer plants the seeds at the right time of year. He plows, plants, fertilizes and receives nothing in advance. He works with Nature because he knows that she will repay him. Depending upon the amount of effort and the quality of work put in, Nature takes over and provides the harvest, a crop that far exceeds the number of seeds planted. Nature goes the extra mile to provide when the labor and effort is applied. It is a law that we are continually reminded of and we see the plentiful fish, the varieties and rebirth of birds, the amazing regeneration and beauty of trees, the incredible burst of color in flowers each Spring ; in everything that She gives us.

ADOPT THIS NOW

This is a philosophy of ethics in human relationships. If we can instill this in children, we will lead them to harmony and understanding and sympathy for those who are weak and unfortunate. It takes us to the adage "I am my brother's keeper." When this becomes a practice, great personal rewards will be experienced.

With all of my heart, I believe this to be true. I have seen it in my own life as this strong belief and philosophy in my parents rewarded them with solid, loving family relationships and loyalties. Their material wealth grew as did their ability to cope with the character building tests of Nature. All families experience difficulty, but to pull together in a time of crisis is a true test of love and commitment. Often, In my own life, I reap the rewards of past efforts and kindnesses. Even the students who visit me years after leaving my classroom help me to reinforce this philosophy that I believe to be so true. I am overwhelmed with the generosity of Nature and the blessings that are sent my way.

Virgil School has a wonderful tradition to reinforce this philosophy. Each day, the person who has presented the morning announcements, completes them by adding "Remember, here at Virgil, we always do our best and do what's right." It is heard each day. It can and will become part of the "consciousness" of both staff and students.

There are Rewards!

In my year of Teacher's College, I met my dynamic, incredibly talented associate drama teacher at Grantham Secondary School. Maureen did everything in her power to build me up and help me to become enthusiastic and motivated while teaching her students. When she left for her maternity leave, I was able to stay on and she continued to tutor me. She went the "extra mile" for me and became one of my lifelong mentors and advocates. She is among the special handful of friends that I have been blessed to share my life with. She still builds me up and makes me feel special. Her kindness and friendship have lasted almost thirty years and I'm proud to call her "friend". She is one of the blessings that come from the place that rewards you for your efforts. Thank you Maureen. This one's for you!

The rule of "Going the Extra Mile" is a promise that exists in the lives of those who practice the law of charity and kindness. I have read countless stories of men and women who, through the struggles of ignorance and poverty, rose above it all by living this principle. It is a solid value that should be taught to children of all ages and I encourage you to implement this lesson into your own life and into the life of your students.

RESPONSIBILITY   Joanne D'Alton Clancy

"Too often, in late years, with jobs fairly easy to come by, workers have the fixed notion that the 'world owes them a living.' They need only to do the minimum, watching the clock, killing time and energy until that moment when the hour hand says another day of labor is finished.

What they fail to realize is that the laws of the Universe require an individual to do his best, utilizing all that is good within him, in order to lead a satisfying, nonboring existence. If he doesn't cooperate in this respect, he is in for trouble, for which he can only blame himself.

You must have experienced the gratifying and exhilarating sensation of time well-spent, after giving your best to the job at hand...of having specific direction to your life...perfect relaxation of mind and body at the end of a day.

However, if you are one of those always complaining, always searching, always fed up with life in general, look to yourself for reevaluation. Perhaps you'll find it's you who owes the world a living - not vice versa."

"Teach a child the benefits of rendering more service and better service than that which is customary, and you will have made contributions of character to that child which will serve him or her all through life."

Napoleon Hill

CHAPTER TWENTY-TWO
BUILDING SELF-ESTEEM

The last chapter that I will be writing in this book is one of my favorite goals. I have always tried to make this a priority in my classroom and have spent years taking courses, reading books and practicing various methods to build my knowledge of "how to build self esteem in children". I hope that I have not just concentrated on children, because it is my firm belief that, when it comes to self esteem, we never grow out of needing it. As educators, there are many opportunities for us to congratulate each other, to reinforce each other's efforts and achievements and to send little notes of encouragement. Unfortunately, it seems that only a handful of teachers on each staff have the courage and insight to practice this. I am astounded at the amount of jealousy and indifference that I have viewed in the teaching profession.

Why do some teachers feel so insecure that they cannot congratulate another for a job "well done"?

Why should we feel the need to hold back our true feelings when congratulating our peers?

Teachers do not get a lot of positive feedback and yet, they, as a whole, need to be encouraged and praised the most.

In my early years, it was my experience when asked to "do a musical", that some of the staff began to resent me and the efforts that I was making to "do my job". As a young person trying to coordinate a "sixty children" musical, I ran into many obstacles, most of them created by other teachers. It was always a puzzle to me why my own peers could not supply the support I needed in a positive manner. Often, it was given begrudgingly and with much criticism, both in front of me and behind my back. I know that I was not alone in this dilemma because I have spoken to many music teachers who have experienced this very same thing. The oddest thing, however, was, that on the night of the performance, when all went well and the children had experienced a successful educational experience, everyone got in line to accept the well-deserved praise of the community. **Everyone!**

I am venting here because I believe that the last chapter combined with this one should be a mandatory focus for many teachers. I use the word "many" because there are just as many of you out there who do practice positive encouragement and who are willing to "go the extra mile". You are the special ones who should be congratulated. You know who you are and I encourage you to "keep up the good work"!

I cannot stress this enough...

TEACHERS MUST ENCOURAGE EACH OTHER, THEY MUST BUILD EACH OTHER UP AND THEY ARE JUST AS RESPONSIBLE FOR BUILDING SELF ESTEEM IN EACH OTHER AS THEY ARE FOR BUILDING SELF ESTEEM IN THEIR STUDENTS!!

This is a difficult profession. It has many rules and regulations. It does not come with clearly outlined lesson plans in the life skill areas that are often the most important. There are few awards and even fewer "award shows". There is a lot of work and effort provided by we teachers that is unseen and unknown. This profession is constantly criticized by a large majority of politicians, businessmen and others in the community who are ignorant of its true value and commitment.

The hours are long and the workload often creeps into the wee hours of the morning. Courses offered in the summers are well attended and used to "better a teacher's skills" rather than provide a bigger paycheck. Vacations are well-deserved and required to prevent "burn out". (There is a growing percentage of "burn out" and you must protect yourself from that.)

The list goes on and on and on...Be prepared for that! AND be prepared to support others who have had the courage to travel on this professional journey alongside of you. It takes courage, stamina, love and commitment to become a good teacher and that's just the beginning. Do you not think that it is time to encourage those walking beside you rather than block their efforts or make them feel somewhat inadequate?

Think of your friends and who you surround yourself with. Are they positive people who make you feel good? Do they talk about others and complain a lot?

I am not telling you to change your friends, I am asking you to evaluate those with whom you associate to see if they are your "builders of success". I consider one of my greatest blessings to be the wonderful friends that I have grown older with. It is clear that they, along with my family, have become my greatest gifts in life. I spend a great deal of time with my mom and sisters as well as my own children and husband. I maintain a handful of friendships and they have been solid, spanning over many years. I do not make friends easily or quickly as I believe that the process is one of time and trust. I surround myself only with those who "build and support" my life and values and I do my best to provide that in return.

Pat comes to mind when I think of a friend who has been around forever. As a young teenager, I looked after her boys and now my daughter babysits her grandchildren. Our friendship has spanned over 35 years and I am grateful for this solid friend who has always supported and built me up, sustaining me in difficult times. We have raised children, traveled on separate paths and experienced different tragic events during those years and, through it all, we knew that there was a bond of friendship that could be utilized at any time. We have had waves and lulls of contact but always true friendship. Pat is always there when I need her and I hope to always do the same for her. We are now in a period of our lives where we see each other regularly and have an ongoing social and personal relationship. Her children have grown up and have children of their own and mine have all reached the teenage years. The gap is closing and there is a more common ground, once again. Thanks, Pat!

Friends require time, energy and love. They should never be abused or misused. They are your refuge from the storms of life and your partners in sharing the celebrations of that same life. They are diverse and complicated, requiring encouragement, support and the constant knowledge that you will always be there for them. Be there for them, build their self esteem and, from that experience, learn to build the self esteem of those with whom you share a career. Your path with be much more pleasant and productive, I promise you!

This is such an important component of maintaining and creating a solid foundation for an effective teaching profession. I would like to see the whole thing "get more positive". Come back to becoming a team and don't allow outside influences to hurt you as a group.

Stick together, stand up for yourselves, make no excuses and promise yourself that "you will make a positive difference on your staff." Be the one that builds and praises. Make the commitment that, in my sister's words "If you can't say anything good, don't say anything at all". Find something good to say and say it!!

MEET DON WOLFE AND ROBERT ALLEN

In 1992, my husband and I had the opportunity of attending a seven day seminar provided by the WIN Institute of California held on Shelter Island, California. It was created and taught by two extraordinary men who came from two totally different backgrounds. We had met these individuals in Seattle, Washington a few months before and were intrigued by their mission to not only create self esteem in people but also to develop Builders of Self Esteem who would carry on and teach others their principles. Since I was a teacher and my husband had always hired crews for the work that he was involved in, we both realized the importance of the human need to feel good and important. We also realized that it was not just a need for children, but for we adults, who seem to be constantly battered by life's difficulties and challenges.

Donald S. Wolfe has an M.A. in Psychology and draws his experience from years of researching and teaching in the fields of family therapy, education, visual imagery, martial arts, personal development seminars and life.

Robert Allen is a three-time best-selling author who has achieved his success in real estate. He believes that real wealth is the ability to understand the inherent gifts that are uniquely yours and to use them to naturally expand your financial, emotional and spiritual world.

Both men are deeply committed to expanding the principles of real wealth and enriched self esteem to as many people as possible, knowing that this will ultimately make our world a far more loving, supportive and harmonious place to live. It is a "line by line, precept upon precept" theory that is used widely throughout the world.

WinKids was intense! We survived twelve hour learning days filled with life-changing exercises, games and workshops. We met many strong, influential leaders including Jack Canfield, who shared valuable teaching methods and tools with this group of eighty. There were participants from every profession including lawyers,

209

homemakers, doctors, business owners, teachers and people in the trades. There were "kids" of all ages ranging from eighteen to eighty who had traveled from both the east and west coast of United States as well as Canada and its bordering states to attend. Authors and teachers in specialized fields shared life experiences and accomplishments. It was thrilling to be in the company of so many people who shared the same desires and goals and who were willing to share the "stumbling blocks" and hurtles of life that had brought them there. We worked with a group of children from San Diego, one of whom still writes to me today and tells of her accomplishments and goals. Thanks Tianna!

From this course, we continued our journey of Building Self Esteem by holding workshops for Kids of All Ages. Many distraught, frightened children became transformed, gaining self-worth and confidence over the day. They pledged to become "winners" who would try to see things in a more positive light and utilize this view to better their lives. Some of these children went on to become better students, less "afraid" to try new things.

WinKids was a life-changing experience for me and I wish to share some of its fundamental lessons with you in the hopes that its principles and teachings will become a part of the self esteem building program in your classroom.

WINKIDS

This chapter is taken from the WINKIDS Corporation and once again, I take no credit for these games, insights and methods. I do however wish to show you the way to own them and make them a part of your teaching. It is with the blessing of these two powerful teachers, Don Wolfe and Robert Allen, that the students of their program are asked to share and continue the process of

BUILDING SELF ESTEEM

Everything you do is an attempt to feel good about who you are and what you are going through. This is true for each and every one of us.

This chapter will look at what you wish to teach your students, but, upon reading it carefully, it will pertain to you, the teacher, as well.

Self esteem means
-being able to experience all parts of yourself and knowing that who you are is a process that continually changes. Self esteem means that there is a value in "everything" that you experience.

YOU ARE VALUABLE. Know that this is true.

Self esteem means
- to be able to feel lonely, rejected, angry, hurt, doubtful, afraid and distrustful for as long as you need to have that experience, knowing that there is always more to you.

Self esteem requires
-the ability to process yourself paradoxically. You are both good and bad, right and wrong, afraid and confident, sad and happy, loved and rejected, quick and slow, discouraged and hopeful, a loser and a winner. All of it is **all** right.

Too many of us feel that we are not allowed to have negative feelings and that is not true at all. Those feelings are a part of us and they need to have their place. We must learn that they should not, however, control our lives even though they are a significant part of our character. By allowing them to have "their time", you are giving yourself the opportunity to vent, be angry or disillusioned and then move on to the more positive building of solutions and avenues that will make you feel stronger and valuable.

The goal of building self esteem is to allow your students to become more successful in all areas of their lives. It is important for them to feel confident, deal with their frustrations and support and appreciate themselves and others more fully. Our goal is to build "winners".

CHILDREN MUST BE WILLING TO COMMIT TO THESE RULES

There are rules that children have to follow before you delve into these exercises and it is important that they agree to follow them. I have found that they are intrigued when we discuss this at the outset and are very willing to follow the rules. I have often mixed two classes together when practicing some of these exercises in order to change their comfort level somewhat. Team teach with another teacher who is willing to spend some time on this with you. I assure you that you will reap many benefits when you do.

1. Be willing to learn from students you may not know well.
2. Learn something unique from everyone you meet.
3. Stand up when sharing.
4. Acknowledge all student successes with hearty, positive applause.
5. Delay any judgement. Be open to learning in a new and different way.
6. You don't have to like it. Just do it!
7. Be willing to stretch outside your comfort zone.
8. Be wise. Be kind. Be respectful to others.
9. Participate fully. Give 100%.
10. Remember - the more you give; the more you get!

Children need to understand that they will be taking "reasonable risks" during the following games and lessons. They may feel uncomfortable or "shy". Being "shy" is not a hereditary characteristic and should not be accepted or used as an excuse. Children must also realize that they can learn to teach their brain that it can learn new things, that it can remember and that it can take their beliefs and make them real.

Just a factual note about your brain

There are two primary parts of your brain that operate very differently. One could be called the *left brain*, your logical mind, your critical or your *conscious mind*. This is the part of you that labels, evaluates, judges, and defines your experiences.

The other part of the brain could be called the *right brain*, your imagination, or your *subconscious mind*. This is the part of the brain that really doesn't know the difference between what is imagined and what is real. When you dream at night, this is the part of your mind that is functioning. When you imagine or feel something, this is the part of your mind that makes it real in your body and produces matching sensations in your body. How many times have you awakened from a dream and actually felt fear or nausea, grateful to realize that it wasn't real, even though it felt so real! The portion of your brain that creates those reactions has the intelligence to control your heart, breathing, blinking of your eyes and other reflex actions that your body performs. This is the part of the brain where your old memories, labels, beliefs, and feelings are learned and stored. **This is the most powerful part of your brain.** It will automatically control your behavior, feelings, and self-esteem. You can learn to control it and make it your ally. You must learn to control this computer and have it obey your thoughts and directions.

Let's Look at Winners and Losers!

There are two prevalent attitudes by which people categorize themselves.

*Loser thoughts
These are people who tend to see themselves as victims. They look at the world in a negative way. They see the cup ½ empty. They get stuck in their negative beliefs:

"I'm shy."
"I can't learn."
"I'm unattractive."
"I'm not good at sports."
"Nobody likes me."

ONCE A PERSON TAKES ON THE LOSER ATTITUDE, HE WILL TEND TO FEEL EVIDENCE AND REASONS TO SUPPORT HIS LIMITING BELIEFS OF HIMSELF IN THE WORLD.

*Winner thoughts
A winner's attitude is quite different. They see the cup ½ full. Problems become opportunities, and they enjoy improving themselves. They are willing to make mistakes because they understand that it is a way to learn to improve. A winner's attitude carries with it confidence, energy, commitment and a feeling of being all right the way they are. A winner knows that there is always the potential to improve and so they continue to learn.

Winners are great learners.

Losers find little value in what they are learning.

Your goal is to set children up to be winners.

Loser Thoughts

I am stuck with who I am.
I don't believe that I can change.
My past determines my future
I can't do it!

Winner thoughts

I accept who I am.
I know that I can learn, change and grow.
I can learn from my past, and can choose to be
different in the future.
I can do it!
I can learn to do it!

WINNERS ARE GREAT LEARNERS.
LEARNERS ARE GREAT LEADERS.
WINNERS ARE GREAT LEADERS.

A Gifted Individual who was a real Winner!!

I met a gifted young man while teaching at NPCC. I believe that Eric was born with severe cerebral palsy among other things. Not having had the opportunity of teaching Eric, my knowledge of his physical disabilities is limited and I apologize for that. My relationship with him began in the morning when he would arrive at school in a horizontal position. He would often lay on his "special" bed in the hallway, waiting for the busy staff to come and prepare him for the day's classes. Eric was a master of blonde jokes and, even though my roots were no longer blonde, the fact that I had once been a natural blonde did come up in our conversation.

Each morning, Eric would have a new "blonde joke" ready for me and he would take great delight in holding back the punch line for just a few seconds, knowing that I would not be able to solve the riddle. We shared many jokes and stories and I appreciated his quick sense of humor.

Some children would find this "hall parking" a hardship and get frustrated at having to wait, but Eric always used it as a time to socialize with those working around him.

This is just one tiny example of how his positive outlook on life inspired others, peers and staff alike, and we recognized just how fortunate we were and how equally successful Eric was. He took his disability and pushed it aside, preventing it from taking over his life and ideas. Eric excelled at everything he pursued. I was amazed to find, one year, that Eric was running a successful business at the Center, hiring students to do the work that he could not physically participate in. With the help of a creative, patient staff (especially Sandra and Bev), he developed illustrations and logos on the computer. These were transferred to his variety of cards and notes that were packaged and sold. Eric attended a local high school part-time and achieved academic excellence. After the required years at NPCC, he graduated and went on to study at Brock University.

I think what impressed me most about Eric was his fearless look at life. He was well aware of his physical restrictions and yet he always pushed forward. He was not afraid to discuss death as he knew it's prematurity was inevitable and it's looming threat hung over him like a cloud. He had made a personal resolution to live his life to the fullest before leaving this planet. His death in his early twenties, left many mourning the spirit of a true warrior. A wonderful video was created to celebrate his life and achievements.

I see Eric as a success story. This young man accomplished more in his short life than many who live to the ripe old age of ninety. He fought for everything he desired to accomplish and achieved it. Eric achieved more than many of us who are physically and emotionally **able** but who are afraid to risk - what?

Eric was a true winner. To me, he personifies the definition of "winner". Thanks, Eric!

"Winners are those people who make a habit out of doing things that losers are uncomfortable doing."

Ed Foreman

LABELS

How many times have you heard someone say, "I'm just ugly" or "I'm clumsy" or "I am the most unlucky person in the world."?

I know that we have all witnessed someone labeling themselves. We are our own worst enemy when it comes to criticism. No one is harder on us than we are on ourselves.

Now is the time for children to learn that they are not their negative labels.

"Get it now kids, so you don't grow up becoming the labels that you have allowed others to give you." I've probably reiterated this sentence a thousand times to children in my "teacher life" and I still sometimes feel insecure about myself and the labels I was given as a child, teenager and young adult. It's a difficult concept to learn. The difference for me is that I learned it in my late thirties. You can learn it now and teach it to children in their formative years. What a difference a decade (or two) makes!

Play the following game for this lesson. "If you need to use labels, use only the positive ones".

Never condemn the child, only the inappropriate action. Create the following page and hand it out.

EXAM IN YOURSELF

1. Circle the number that best represents where you presently rate yourself on this scale.
2. Transfer the number to the blank at the right
3. Add up the numbers for your total score.
4. Circle the labels that you most want to change.

Shy	0	1	2	3	4	5	6	7	8	9	10	Friendly	_____
Lazy	0	1	2	3	4	5	6	7	8	9	10	Motivated	_____
Clumsy	0	1	2	3	4	5	6	7	8	9	10	Athletic	_____
Poor Memory	0	1	2	3	4	5	6	7	8	9	10	Good Memory	_____
Fearful	0	1	2	3	4	5	6	7	8	9	10	Courageous	_____
Unlucky	0	1	2	3	4	5	6	7	8	9	10	Lucky	_____
Unfeeling	0	1	2	3	4	5	6	7	8	9	10	Caring	_____
Unattractive	0	1	2	3	4	5	6	7	8	9	10	Attractive	_____
Sad	0	1	2	3	4	5	6	7	8	9	10	Happy	_____
Stupid	0	1	2	3	4	5	6	7	8	9	10	Smart	_____
Angry	0	1	2	3	4	5	6	7	8	9	10	Loving	_____
Lonely	0	1	2	3	4	5	6	7	8	9	10	Popular	_____
Insecure	0	1	2	3	4	5	6	7	8	9	10	Confident	_____
Tense	0	1	2	3	4	5	6	7	8	9	10	Relaxed	_____
												Total	_____

Use this lesson to seriously look at the meaning of each of these adjectives and how they can affect us when used as labels. Have students share examples and ideas. Don't share results individually but use the results for each child to look at their own views of what they see and wish to change in themselves. It wakes them up a bit and they will talk about it to their friends later on.

Winners know that they are not their negative labels

Discussing the results of "the exam"

"We learn to define and label ourselves and the world through our experiences. We use labels to describe who we are to ourselves and others. Labels might also be called beliefs. The labels that we use to describe ourselves, will either restrict us from growing or empower us to get better. We are all diamonds in disguise. We just need to remove the labels, beliefs, and thoughts that keep us from shining." WinKids

The score that was achieved in the Exam in Yourself exercise represents how you have learned to see yourself. This judgement or label is not necessarily the "real" you. You have just learned to see yourself this way from past experiences and reinforcement of these experiences by yourself and others. Just as you have learned to have these labels, you can learn to have new ones.

If you scored above 70, you tend to see yourself in a powerful, positive light.

If you scored under 70, you need to learn to see yourself in a more powerful and positive light because: _____

_____

Note the labels that you want to change and realize that **"The more you can accept the way you presently are, the easier it is to become someone new."** It is important for us to look honestly at our faults and failings in order to improve upon them or get rid of them altogether.

I have always had a very vivid imagination. As a child, I know that I made up stories because often, I wished that I could be someone else or do other things. I dreamed of living in a bigger city and becoming a movie star. I thought I would become a concert pianist or a dancer. As a young child, I dealt with some ridicule because I wore special shoes for awhile and I couldn't always play the sports that the other kids played so I would make up stories to cover my inadequacies. They took me to different places and I enjoyed being there.

As I grew older, I had to take a serious look at my bad habit. It was very difficult for me to acknowledge my weakness but, slowly, I began trying harder and harder to tell more accurate stories. Today, many years later, I am noted for telling the truth and I always make a special effort to include accurate details or actual quotes to add credibility to the things that I say. Am I proud of my weakness? Of course not. It's just one of many. I'm sure that I hurt people in my youth along the way but I have to hope that they, too, had faults that they worked to improve and had to rely on the forgiveness of their benefactors. We cannot hold grudges or carry the burden of anger for years because someone else hurt us. They are on this journey just like you and I and we must all work together to "forgive and forget" or it will be our own undoing if we cannot. After having gone through a difficult period of time with someone, I was finally able to forgive but I no longer wished to associate with that person. I learned that just because you have been able to come to the point of forgiving someone, it does not necessarily mean that you have to re-instate the friendship or relationship. Forgiveness is key but happiness is the ultimate key and their presence in your life may not bring happiness. Sometimes it is more important to learn the lesson, forgive the act and move on at your comfort level. This may or may not include the person responsible for the difficulties that you encountered. Be fair to yourself as well.

This "label" lesson is just the beginning in giving children the excuse to begin the process right now rather than much later in their lives. Learning to be honest enough to accept our frailties and creating the desire to strengthen them is a very mature lesson in life.

GAMES TO BUILD SELF ESTEEM

This section of the chapter will introduce you to a number of games that can be used by "kids of all ages." It is sometimes fun to practice them with a group of friends before venturing into the classroom with them. Play fair and be honest. Try to look at life through the eyes of a child; through the eyes of your childhood and see what you can come up with.

"Tradition whispers that in the sky is a bird, blue as the sky itself, which brings to its finder happiness. But everyone cannot see it; for mortal eyes are prone to be blinded by wealth, fame, and position, and deceived by the mocking Will-o-Wisp of empty honors. But for the fortunate ones who seek with open eyes and hearts, with the artlessness, simplicity, and faith which are richest in childhood, there is an undying promise; and to them the Blue Bird lives and carols, a rejoicing symbol of Happiness and Contentment unto the end."

From the "New Psychology."

What's the Difference between a Winner and a Loser?

Game #1

- Write down a situation where you feel like a loser and a victim.
- Write down how you would view the same situation from the eyes of a Superkid, who is a winner.
- Share your insights.

This creates a very interesting class discussion. The victims become fairly evident and you can begin to work towards a "winner" outlook and program.

Game #2

Winners (people with good self-esteem) are willing to look foolish. Introduce yourself to three different people in a foolish way.

Game #3

Practice experiencing negative feelings by whining to several people about something that is bothering you. The person listening may respond accordingly.

Game #4

Have students make a colorful, clear label that states "I'M AN INCREDIBLE LEARNING MACHINE."
They must wear that label all day (or more if you wish).
They have to see it, tell others about it and begin to take the information in. They should see it and read it aloud whenever they look in a mirror. Conviction will break the block.
Explain the roles of the brain to them. Tell them of its ability to "do as it's told."

A Spelling Game to reinforce Game #4
- Find a Learner who considers him or herself to be a poor speller.
- Have the Learner spell out loud the word:
  M E T A M O R P H O S I S
- Write down the word correctly and clearly so that it can be seen by the Learner
- Learner takes the time to transfer the written word into a word clearly seen in the mind's eye.
- Add color to the word.
- Spell out loud from your mental image going from the written word to the mental word and back until it's correct and mentally locked in.
- Then spell it backwards until it's correct
- Spell it forwards with conviction.

Learners can open and close their eyes to create a visual image for themselves.

Game #5

Write a "braggy" paragraph or three about your positive qualities. Don't hold back!
The teacher should make a list on the board (with or without class input but again, I like those vocabulary lessons) of many positive qualities. Ex. Friendly, motivated, athletic, loving etc.

Game #6 My Name Is Powerful

Make a positive acronym with your first and last name. Have students use a thesaurus and create a fun, vocabulary lesson at the same time.

INCREDIBLE   Have children create a poster with their acronym
NICE   Display them in the classroom or hall.
GENEROUS   Don't allow children to be embarrassed
RESOURCEFUL
IMPRESSIVE
DRAMATIC

A Game of Emotions

Each of us experience different emotions at different times of the day or even during an hour. Sometimes we are in a great mood and happy when someone comes along and says something rude or offensive. Instantly, we become angry and irritable.

How long do we stay in this state of anger? How many people do we tell? Do we dwell on it for a long time? These are questions that many of us answer with a "YES - he/she made me mad."

Do you like the way you feel? My guess is NO, so here's the Plan. No one makes you angry! That's right! It's your choice!

"WHATEVER YOU'RE FEELING - IT'S YOUR CHOICE!"

Allow yourself to step purposely into other parts of yourself and experience the changes that you feel. Try to remember an experience that made you angry and focus on it.

Game #7

Have a CD player ready with a CD of quiet music.
Give your students the emotion of angry to begin with.
Put the music on.
Have students move around the room in an angry fashion until you stop the music and give them another emotion - caring.
Movement in a very caring way begins and the anger disappears.
The next break gives them the emotion of silly and the room erupts in silliness.
This game can be carried on for as many emotions as you wish to deal with at a time.
Use emotions like elated, sad, angry, confused, bored, depressed, frustrated, judgmental, shy, forgiving, intelligent...
The ultimate lesson here is that "you have the ability to change your emotions at will." You can replace a negative emotion with a positive one whenever you choose. Just focus on another time, thing, or place.
Students of all ages love this game and I use it in the classroom whenever we need a break or a "fun" time. It not only relieves tension, but it allows children to act out feelings in a very informal and non-threatening way.
Discuss the values of being able to shift out of a negative emotion and how much better you can feel if you choose.

Find your Inner Strength

There is an inner strength within us. It should determine our limits. It knows our beliefs, morals and values and should be strong enough to ward off potential disasters in our lives. Children don't have to be followers when they are taught to be positive leaders and role models. In our travels, we will meet the student who is a leader but uses his talents in a negative way. Our purpose is to teach him/her to use those leadership skills to be a positive leader.

Game #8
Be prepared to spend at least one hour on this game.
Have each individual make a mask from a paper plate.
You could make one too, if you wish.

223

On one side, they write their fears of what other children could say or do to them. This becomes the outside of the plate.

On the inside of the plate, they write the truth, the real things that they **are** to invalidate the outer comments.

Example: the outside says   The inside says

"You're a fraidy cat"   "I have courage. I don't have to fight to prove myself."

Have each child read the inside comments, study them and practice reading them aloud to themselves.

The plate should be filled on both sides with true feelings written in bold letters This exercise requires trust and should be used later on in the year when children are more confident to be honest among their peers. There will be some surprises for you, the teacher, as you see the fears of some of those seemingly confident children come out.

To begin the exercise, choose one strong, confident student to sit in the middle of a small circle of peers. His/her peers read the comments written on the outside of the mask while the child on the hot seat reads the inside comments in a louder voice to drown out the voices around him/her. Be sure to supervise the exercise carefully so as not to allow badgering or too much discomfort. Have the child read the inside comments until you feel positive that they are no longer affected by the group.

This is a powerful game and should be played later on in the year when children are comfortable with their peers. Choose your player carefully. You may not be able to have every child in the class be the "middle man" but, if you can, go for it!

Things get pretty noisy but also very interesting as you watch the yelling and dramatic actions of the children. Confidence is being built and both sides should clearly understand that they are not ridiculing, but actually, helping their classmate in the"hot seat" grow stronger and develop an ability to overcome any fears that they may have.

"Did you realize that you can change old fears just as easily as you learned them?"

Again we discuss Reasonable Risks

224

In order to build confidence, there must be a willingness to take reasonable risks. It is an obvious fact that teachers must provide a safe, positive environment for learning.

Too often, children are afraid to ask questions. They believe that;

-other children will think that they're "stupid".

- the teacher will think less of them if they didn't "get it".

-it's embarrassing to admit that you didn't understand the point of the lesson.

Often, children would rather fail than admit to not having understood the lesson because it's easier and won't draw attention to them.

As confidence levels are boosted, it becomes much more clear to them that everyone should ask questions. With self esteem comes courage and an ongoing trust in building relationships with teachers and peers. As teachers practice the building of self esteem with their students, they are building bridges and bonds to develop the trust that is required to move further and further ahead into the "risk zone". Asking questions during class definitely enters the category of taking reasonable risks.

If you actually taught a lesson on asking questions at the beginning of the school year, you could discuss all of the issues of the fears and apprehensions that children face. This introduces the fears right at the beginning and allows children to face them head on. As a class you could make a series of rules regarding appropriate question asking.

When Should You ask a Question?

1) If, at any point during the lesson, you do not fully understand the concept, ask a question.

    Remember that often, if you don't understand something, there is a good chance that someone else is having difficulty understanding it as well. You usually represent those who are more timid in asking. You are helping to clarify the point for others as well as yourself.

2) If the teacher has saved a time near the end of the lesson for any questions, write yours down and save it for that time. Perhaps it will be answered before the end of the lesson. If not, ask it when the time is right. Learn to access and trust your intuition.

3) Often teachers will review the points presented. Perhaps there will be a helpful summary which will clarify your difficulty. Wait until the end before you ask.

4) If there is an unclear point that is crucial to moving ahead in the lesson, raise your hand to question that point. The teacher will get to you at the correct time.

5) No question is a "wrong question" Be prepared to accept all questions, even if they seem silly or irrelevant to you.

6) Be very understanding of the fact that each child has the right to feel safe. Each time someone takes a risk and asks a question, respect them and allow the answer to be given in a supportive manner.

When is a question a stupid question? When you don't ask it!

If you wish, you could discuss the process of asking a question. When children try to plan their questions more carefully, they tend to ask better ones that will be more specific and helpful.

Try to focus on what it is you wish to know and then ask the question. Be specific!

"Getting what you want isn't difficult as long as you're clear about what it is you're looking for."

Mindworks

Visualization is not for everyone but...

Game #9

Brainstorm with children the things that they see for themselves.
Example:
1) passing a math test
2) winning an award
3) overcoming a fear
4) rising to a challenge
5) defeating a competitor

You give directions:
Close your eyes and see yourself as a victor over the challenge. Ask these questions to yourself while your eyes are closed.
1) What did you accomplish?
2) What are you wearing?

3) Are there a lot of people around you?
4) How do you feel?
5) Do you like the way that you feel?

Watch their faces and be sure that they are making a concerted effort in visualizing their accomplishments. The point is to bring them to a realization that these goals can and will be accomplished **if the effort is put forward.**

Game #10 (really, this is more of an exercise or could be part of guidance lessons)

Have students actually write their goals in a book. I encourage journal writing and have always made it a part of my English program. Either keep a separate section for short and long-term goals, time lines and **results** or have a separate duo-tang for goals and accomplishments.

Jack Canfield has an invaluable compilation of exercises that deal with goals and other related activities. They are presented in a very large binder called "Self Esteem in the Classroom". These pages are photocopiable. Choose the most relevant ones for your students and create a booklet for them. As children fill the pages in, you can take them up or mark them individually. Add pages as time and topics allow. When people practice the process of writing their goals down, it becomes a much more clearly defined plan of action. It forces them to become more responsible for implementing and accomplishing them. This goes back to the plan for Success at the beginning of this book. Read it carefully as it applies here.

Game #11

Each child purchases an autograph book. Every once in a while, they autograph a book from the identity of being a Superstar. By the end of the year, each child should have the autographs of at least all of their classmates as well as having provided their own autograph to their peers. It gives importance and relevance to their place in the world. Oddly enough, those autograph books are never thrown out with the other subject notebooks at the end of the year. Journals and personal goal setting books tend to become keepsakes for future perusal. It's true!

A Little Bit of "Canfield" in my Life

I am taking the liberty of sharing some "Self Esteem in the Classroom" with Jack Canfield. This was part of a booklet that was compiled for the Win Institute, San Diego, California, May 11/ 1992.

A very interesting formula for life is

E + R = O
Events + Response = Outcome

If you want new, better outcomes, you have to change your behavior and do something new. It can be risky or scary. Your R (response) is your point of power. Stop blaming events and change your response to create a positive or more satisfying outcome.

Teaching children to change their reactions to events at school can be a turning point in their lives. Students learn from repetition and modeling. For you to be an effective self esteem builder, you yourself must have high self esteem. Don't forget to clearly see your value. Don't accept put-downs. Dare to dream and practice unconditional regard for others.

Always model the use of self-talk.
Replace "I can't" with "I can" or "I won't."
"I'll try" with "I will".
"should" with "want to" or "don't want to"

The B.E.S.T. Pledge

Be the Best that You can be
Believe in Yourself
Stand up for Yourself
Trust Yourself
B.E.S.T.
Be the B.E.S.T. That you can be.

There are many available resources for Building Self Esteem. There is a list compiled by Jack Canfield that will be added at the back of this book as reference material. I urge you to take this Self Esteem Building very seriously. It can change the lives of your students and they will always remember the efforts that you made in helping them to achieve their individual successes. Self Esteem is the cornerstone of what we say and do. It can create leaders or it's lack can create failures. Teaching children to be winners in the true sense of the word is the most valuable lesson that they will ever learn. Over the years, I have watched the course of many of my students' lives develop. It is clear to see where "winner" thoughts have been utilized.

BE A WINNER and TEACH WINNERS!

In the following books, I have found credibility and a renewed enthusiasm for life. I must admit that I haven't always taken an interest in reading these books. In fact, they are part of the extensive collection belonging to my husband Dan, who continuously shares his interest with me and provides me with the support and wealth of knowledge that is found in them. I have always been a very busy person who rarely sits and reads a novel for pleasure, let alone delves into deep philosophy books. Much of my career has been spent reading books for courses or preparing units so I tend to shy away from the "deeper" books when I have the opportunity to "just" read. Dan, on the other hand, derives a great deal of pleasure from reading books written by uplifting authors and I am very grateful that he has been persistent in sharing their value with me. There are many mornings when I awake to headphones being placed on my head as he provides a book on tape for my listening pleasure or some relaxation tape to help get me started in the day. Thanks, Dan!!

A VALUABLE LIST

(1). **"A Way out from In"**, a collection of contemplative essays which range over the full gamut of human experiences. It is compiled by Joanne D'Alton Clancy and published by Clancy Publications

(2). **"You, Inc."** is described as the Ten Principles to dramatically Increase your Wealth. I use this book in the classroom to build upon the "wealth" of children's abilities and habits. With a little adapting, it is an invaluable tool to teach children of all ages. This book was written by Burke Hedges and published by INTI Publishing, Tampa, Florida. It provides a very systematic and clear approach to building "oneself".

(3). **"Energizing the 12 Powers of Your Mind"** is written by Napoleon Hill. It shows you, step-by-step, exactly how to attain your highest goals in clear, easy-to-follow language. What a wonderful way to discover the "power within you". Published by Leisure Books.

(4). **"The Master-Key To Riches"** by Napoleon Hill describes in step-by-step detail today's greatest practical philosophy of success and shows you how to succeed in any walk of life. Fawcett Publications.

(5). **"Key to Yourself"** by Dr. Venice Bloodworth contains many teachings that will unlock the dreams and talents within in order to realize and build success. Last publication, Scrivener and Company, 1977.

(6). **"Mindworks - Unlock the Promise Within"** is an NLP Book by Anne Linden. It provides NLP Tools for Building a Better Life. Andrews McMeel Publishing.

(7). **"Self Esteem in the Classroom: A Curriculum Guide"** by Jack Canfield. Available from Self Esteem Seminars, 6035 Bristol Parkway, Suite C, Culver City, CA 90230

(8). **"100 Ways to Enhance Self-Concept in the Classroom"** by Jack Canfield and Harold Wells. Englewood, Cliffs, NJ: Prentice-Hall, 1976

(9). **"Inviting School Success"** by William Purkey and John Novak. Bedmont, CA : Wadsworth, 1984

(10). **"Cooperative Discipline"** by Linda Albert. Circle Pines, MN: AGS, 1989

(11). **"Peoplemaking"** by Virginia Satir. Science and Behavior Books, Inc., 1972

(12). **"How to Read a Book"** The Classic Guide to Intelligent Reading written by Mortimer J. Adler and Charles Van Doren, published by Simon and Schuster, 1972

Ingrid U. Hearn

About the Author:

Ingrid Hearn has been a teacher most of her life. She is a mother of three and has experienced the difficulties of raising a family while teaching full-time. She brings her accumulated knowledge from countless sources to the written page and hopes to share her "learning mistakes" with other educators. In her book, she praises those who teach and shares personal insights with meaningful examples of the many aspects of the teaching profession. Ingrid is presently a music/drama director and has created a motivational lecture series, "Learn with Hearn", for Faculties of Education and School Boards. Her wit and enthusiasm are evident in her lectures and in her book. Her goal is to praise and support the teaching profession, as she believes it to be one of the most valuable gifts that we in the present have to offer those of the future. "The lives of precious children are in our hands and we must do everything in our power to provide them with the tools to build a positive and purposeful future."

Printed in the United States
879800005BA